EASY GUIDE TO BRIDGE

CADOGAN BRIDGE SERIES

In this series:

REESE, T.
Brilliancies and Blunders in the European Bridge Championship

FLINT, J. & NORTH, F.
Tiger Bridge Revisited

REESE, T. & BIRD, D.
Famous Hands from Famous Matches

SMITH, N.
Bridge Literature

SENIOR, B.
Bread and Butter Bidding

WANG, CHIEN-HWA
The Squeeze at Bridge

RIGAL, B.
Test your Bridge Judgement

For a complete catalogue of Cadogan Bridge books (which includes the former Maxwell Macmillan Bridge list) please write to:

Cadogan Books, London House, Parkgate Road, London SW11 4NQ
Tel: (0171) 738 1961   Fax: (0171) 924 5491

EASY GUIDE TO BRIDGE

ALAN and MAUREEN HIRON

LONDON, NEW YORK

CADOGAN BOOKS DISTRIBUTION

UK/EUROPE/AUSTRALASIA/ASIA/AFRICA
Distribution: Grantham Book Services Ltd, Isaac Newton Way, Alma Park
Industrial Estate, Grantham, Lincs NG31 9SD.
Tel: (01476) 67421:   Fax: (01476) 590223.

USA/CANADA/LATIN AMERICA/JAPAN
Distribution: Paramount Distribution Center, Front and Brown Streets,
Riverside, New Jersey 08075, USA.
Tel: (609) 461 6500:   Fax: (609) 764 9122.

First Published 1994 by Cadogan Books plc, London House, Parkgate
Road, London SW11 4NQ

Reprinted 1995

Briish Library Cataloguing in Publication Data
A CIP catalogue record for this book is available from the British Library.

ISBN 1-85744-509-0

Typeset by Tim Kennemore.
Cover design by Brian Robins.
Printed and bound in Great Britain by BPC Wheatons Ltd, Exeter.

Contents

Introduction

Why play bridge?

Why bother to learn what is generally accepted as the most difficult and demanding of all card games?

Perhaps, because some thirty million plus people worldwide already do. And that number is growing daily.

We can think of few other competitive games that all age groups can play on equal terms throughout their lives.

And none as enjoyable.

Visit virtually anywhere; it's odds-on that you can rapidly get directions to the nearest bridge club and soon have thirteen cards in your hand.

As a bridge player, you need never be lonely. Or bored. Or lack mental stimulation.

And it is a game where you learn something new every time you play.

About the Authors

Alan and Maureen Hiron have collaborated on a number of books—and not just on bridge. They have written best-selling quiz books and also scripted the questions for TV quiz shows, such as *Fifteen to One*.

Alan Hiron

Alan was the Head Master of the famous London School of Bridge for nearly thirty years. Originally a mathematician, he then worked with computers for a number of years, before switching almost entirely to a literary career.

He is the bridge correspondent to the *Independent* and the *Independent on Sunday*, and a former editor of *Bridge* Magazine—the world's oldest. Alan has won all the major British bridge events at least once, and has represented both England and Great Britain, both as player and non-playing captain.

In 1990 he won the inaugural World Senior Pairs Championship, and in partnership with Maureen, his wife, took the bronze medal for the Senior Pairs in the 1993 European Community Championships.

Maureen Hiron

Maureen has also represented England and Great Britain at bridge, but is perhaps best known as an inventor of games.

Her first, invented in 1982, was *Continuo*, which became a British bestseller that year and is now a firm favourite in some thirty countries. Others quickly followed, such as *Quadwrangle*, *Quizwrangle*, *Cavendish* and *Chip In*, and she now concentrates on expanding her Rhino range of card games (RHINO—anagram of HIRON!) which include *DUO*, *77*, *Croque*, *Teddy's Party* and *Black Rhino*—though she is the first to admit that none of them can compete with bridge!

1

Tricks and Trumps

The ideas of trumps and winning tricks will be familiar to anyone who plays whist or solo—if you are at home with either of these games you can skip rapidly through this chapter. In case you are not, it is absolutely vital that you should grasp these concepts before you can start playing bridge.

Bridge is a game for four players—never three, never five. It is completely a partnership game and—purely for convenience—we shall refer to the four players as:

North

West   East

South

When you actually play, geography does not come into it. It simply allows us to refer to 'North' instead of 'the player whose cards are written down at the top of the diagram'. The players facing one another across the table are partners, North with South and East with West. If a player does something good and wins some points to enter on the scoresheet, his partner benefits by just as much. Equally, if a player does something foolish and loses a lot of points, no matter how unnecessarily, his partner suffers to the same extent. As we said, it is completely a partnership game.

A complete pack of 52 cards is used for play (no jokers) and in each suit the importance of the cards is the same: Ace (which always counts high), King, Queen, Jack (less commonly nowadays called the knave), ten, nine, eight, seven, six, five, four, three and two.

You will often find that there are two packs of cards on the table when you play but only one is used at a time. The two packs are used alternately as, to save time, one pack is shuffled while the next hand is dealt.

The preliminaries are as follows—assuming that you have found three other players, tables, chairs, etc. One pack is shuffled and spread face downwards, in a line across the table. The four players each draw and face one card. This determines which of the other three will be your partner! The players drawing the two highest cards will be partners, as will the two players drawing lower cards. So if A draws the ace of hearts, B the queen of diamonds, C the five of clubs and D the three of spades, then A will partner B and C will partner D. A problem arises if, say, D's card was the queen of clubs instead—the same rank as B's card. The tie is split by the ranking order of the suits—an order which it is vitally important to commit to memory for the next phase of the game. *Spades are the highest-ranking suit, then hearts, then diamonds, while clubs are the lowest-ranking suit.* So, even with the revised draw, A and B would still be partners.

There is one curiosity—the player who draws the highest card has the choice of seats! So, by 'winning the cut', you can avoid both a possible draught and the rickety kitchen chair that has been brought in to make up the numbers. You also have the privilege of dealing the first hand and choosing which of the two packs (if available) you would like to use. Once you have chosen your seat your partner faces you and your opponents can make their own arrangements.

For each deal that you play there are four distinct stages:

I   The deal
II   The bidding (or auction)
III The play
IV   The scoring

I The deal

Suppose that you won the cut and are to deal the first hand. The player on your left shuffles the pack with which you have chosen to deal and, when he has finished, you pass the pack, face downwards, to the player on your right. He cuts the cards, placing the top half of the pack nearer to you, but does not complete the cut. You pick up the farther half and put it on top of the nearer. Now you deal the cards, one at a time, clockwise, starting with the player on your left. If all goes well, the last card goes to you and everyone has thirteen cards. The idea of cutting is not to prevent cheating but often, while cards are being shuffled, other players may see the bottom card which will end up in your hand.

While you are dealing your partner shuffles the other pack of cards and leaves it, face downwards, on his right-hand corner of the table. ("If you're not demented quite, Put the cards upon your right" is a couplet to remind you. Poetically speaking, its solitary virtue is that it rhymes.)

After the play of the hand you have dealt has been completed and the score agreed, the player on your left picks up the second pack (which he finds on his left) and passes it to his right for you to cut. Then he deals and the process is continued. Note that the partner of the dealer always shuffles the old pack and that the turn of dealing (like so many other things in bridge, as we will see) goes clockwise round the table. This sounds complicated but it soon becomes second nature and the position of the other pack of cards on the table will always tell you whose deal it is.

II The bidding (or auction)
Although this comes before the play of each hand, this (oddly enough) will prove much easier to explain when you have an idea of the play.

III The play
One of the players starts by taking a card from his hand and placing it face-upwards in the middle of the table. He is said to have *led* the card. Clockwise round the table the other three players each contribute a card. This little bundle of four cards is called a *trick* and the trick is won by the player contributing the highest card in the suit that was led. So if the play to the first trick looks like this after West has led:

11

North

♠ K

West   **East**

♠ 2   ♠ 3

South

♠ 7

It will be North's king that wins the trick. He picks up the four cards and puts them face downwards in a neat pile on his edge of the table. There are several important points to note.

i) It is absolutely mandatory to follow suit if it is possible for you to do so. Failure to do so when you could follow suit *(revoking)* incurs severe penalties. If you have no cards in the suit led you must discard something from another suit with (for the time being) no chance of winning the trick. So, if the two of clubs that has been led and you have no clubs, even playing the ace of spades will not help you.

ii) Although the object of the game is to win as many tricks as possible, you are not competing against your partner. It is just as good for your partnership for him to win a trick as you. So, in the example above, even if South held the ace of spades, he would be quite happy to follow with his seven, hoping to score another trick later with his ace. Indeed, if you do win, you do not start a separate pile of tricks—just one pile for tricks won by your side makes it easier to count. If you put the tricks that your side has won in an overlapping row pointing at partner, it is easy to see at all times how many tricks you have scored.

iii) Whichever player it is who wins a trick leads to the next trick. He does not have to play the same suit again but has complete freedom of choice from his remaining cards. Once he has led, of course, the other three players must follow suit if they can.

iv) As everyone has started with thirteen cards, there will be thirteen tricks
to fight for on every deal. Sometimes it will be a close-run thing—perhaps
seven to North-South, six to East-West; sometimes it will be a much
more one-sided affair. Twelve tricks (with only one for the opponents)
is called a *small slam*; all thirteen tricks is called a *grand slam*.

There is another important concept—that of a trump suit—which features in the play of the cards and has to be fully explained before we can
consider the bidding. Before the play starts, one of the four suits can be
chosen as a trump suit. The chosen suit is determined by the bidding.

The cards in the selected trump suit are all-powerful—even the two
of trumps is enough to beat an ace of any of the other three suits. You
have, however, to follow the rules of play at all times—you will only have
the chance of trumping a winner if you have no cards in the suit that was
led. So if, clubs were trumps, West led the king of hearts and North played
the ace of hearts, East could only play his two of clubs if he held no hearts.
He would then win the trick unless South, like him, held no hearts and
decided to play a higher trump. Then the trick would go to South.

It is not obligatory to trump even if you have no cards in the suit led—you
always have the option of discarding a card from another suit (with, of
course, no chance of winning the trick).

The verb to *ruff* is often used as an alternative to *trump*—it means
exactly the same. Both trump and ruff are corruptions of triumph, an old
card game with the features of tricks and trumps as described above.

Sometimes (again depending on the bidding) a hand is played without
a trump suit. Then every trick is won on merit—if you have no cards in
the suit led you cannot possibly win the trick. The hand is said to be played
in *no-trumps*.

IV The scoring

Again, although a score is written down at the conclusion of each hand,
it will be necessary for us to examine what the bidding is all about before
anything about the scoring will be meaningful.

13

2

What is a Bid?

As the object of the game is to win as many tricks as possible, length in trumps is a great help. In whist and similar games the trump suit is chosen by cutting the cards before dealing or, perhaps, turning up the dealer's last card. In bridge the selection of the trump suit is very much more sophisticated. Indeed, it is effectively put up for auction with all four players bidding against one another. The highest bidder chooses the trump suit. (Or, as an alternative, elects that the hand be played in no-trumps.)

The dealer has the first bid in the auction. After that the turn to bid runs clockwise round the table, just like everything else in bridge. Suppose that South, the dealer, finds himself with:

> ♠ AK754
> ♥ 3
> ♦ KQ107
> ♣ AJ5

It is a fair hand in terms of honour cards (aces, kings, queens and jacks—the cards that are most likely to win tricks) and, as he has more cards in spades than any other suit, he would be inclined to suggest spades as trumps. He does so by saying the words "One spade". Now, this does not mean that he could win one trick if spades were trumps (the ace of spades on its own would be enough for that!) but that, with his partner's co-operation, he hopes to make at least one *plus six* tricks out of the thirteen available if they have the advantage of choosing spades as trumps. Note—a *bid* always suggests six more tricks than are named. So a bid of two hearts suggests the possibility of making two plus six (eight) tricks if hearts are trumps. Equally, a bid of seven diamonds hopes to make seven plus six—all thirteen tricks—with partner's help if diamonds are trumps.

Of course South may have dealt himself a hand like this:

♠ 10843
♥ J74
♦ Q92
♣ 983

when, although as before spades is his longest suit, he has little or no expectation of making even seven tricks unless his partner can do something dramatic. South does not have to suggest his best suit—instead he
says *No Bid*. Alternatively, he can say *Pass*. Both calls mean the same
thing and the choice is optional. But be consistent! If you say Pass with
bad hands and No Bid with very bad hands you may (rightly!) be ac-
cused of unethical behaviour.

Next, consider the problem of West who has just heard "One spade"
on his right. With a poor hand it must be right for him to pass but with
fair values and a good heart suit he might try "Two hearts". It has got to
be *two* hearts for this is an auction sale (where you cannot bid £10 or
even £20 over an earlier bid of £20). Now it is the turn of North to bid.
With a poor hand he says No Bid but with values and a diamond suit he
might try three diamonds. He has here the advantage of knowing that his
partner has a fair hand for South *opened the bidding* rather than passing. The auction continues round the table, possibly for several rounds,
until three players in succession say No Bid. You cannot bid against yourself
in an auction, so the three consecutive passes are like "Going, going, gone!"
A possible complete auction might be:

West	North	East	South
			1 ♠
2 ♥	3 ♦	Pass	Pass
Pass			

The only exception to three No Bids ending matters occurs when the dealer and the next two players all pass to start with. It would be unfair on East, with perhaps his best hand of the evening, not to have a chance!

Just because you have passed originally does not mean that you have to keep on passing, so this is another possible auction:

West	North	East	South
Pass	Pass	Pass	1 ♠
2 ♥	3 ♦	Pass	Pass
Pass			

This means that diamonds are trumps, whatever was bid before, and that North-South have set themselves the target of making at least nine out of the thirteen tricks. Should they succeed (and any extra tricks they make are a bonus) they will score points and their opponents will not score anything. Should they fail, they will not score any points at all and their opponents will collect penalty points. The larger the margin by which they fail, the larger the penalty that they incur. So, as the ultimate object of the game is to score more points than your opponents, it can easily become expensive to fall several tricks short of your target rather than let the opponents choose the trump suit. Within reason, you only bid what you think your side has a fair chance of making.

Next, for those of you who have only played whist or solo, some more important ideas and one or two new words. The player who first names the suit that finally becomes trumps is known as the *declarer*. In the auctions above it is North who invented the idea of diamonds as trumps and so he becomes declarer. Once the bidding is over and the declarer determined, the play starts. The player on the left of declarer (in this case East) leads a card and only after he has done so (and not before!) the declarer's partner (here South) spreads his entire hand on the table, face upwards, and becomes known as the *dummy*. He takes no further part whatsoever in the play and has to wait patiently until the hand is over—giving him an ideal opportunity to make the tea or pour the drinks!

16

The declarer is in sole charge of both his own hand and the dummy. So, after East has led, declarer leans forward and plays a card from dummy. West plays a card and then declarer (working twice as hard!) plays from his own hand. The usual rules of play are followed—if a card from dummy wins a trick, a card from dummy must be led to start the next trick; if declarer wins a trick, he must next lead from his own hand.

Remember that we made the point that the first player to name the final trump suit becomes declarer. So if the bidding had gone:

West	North	East	South
			1 ♠
Pass	2 ♠	Pass	Pass
Pass			

it would be South who became declarer and North, after West had led a card, the dummy. It is just possible, if unlikely, that the final trump suit was first bid by an opponent so, to be strictly accurate, we should say that it is the first player of the partnership to bid the final trump suit who becomes declarer. So after:

West	North	East	South
1 ♣	Pass	Pass	2 ♣
Pass	3 ♣	Pass	
Pass	Pass		

although West first bid clubs, it will be South who is declarer.

From what we have said so far it may sound as though the bidding is going to get very high very quickly, especially if all four players are in action—perhaps:

17

West	North	East	South
			1♠
2♥	3♦	4♣ etc.	

Matters are not, however, as bad as they seem. If you remember, when we discussed cutting for partners, we mentioned the ranking order of the suits. *Spades are the highest, then hearts, then diamonds and finally clubs.* This order is of great importance in the bidding as well. A bid of one spade is higher than a bid of one heart (although both contracts will require seven tricks for fulfilment). One heart is higher than one diamond, and so on. So the auction might legitimately start:

West	North	East	South
			1♣
1♦	1♥	1♠	

but if South now wanted to bid his clubs again he would have to call *two* clubs in order to outbid one spade. It may help you to regard all the possible bids as rungs on a ladder starting at the bottom with one club and following with one diamond, one heart, one spade, two clubs and so on up to seven hearts and seven spades at the top.

Finally, as discussed in the chapter on Tricks and Trumps, there is the possibility of a hand being played in *no-trumps*. Players can bid one no-trump, two no-trumps (normally written for convenience as 1NT, 2NT) etc., just as if they were bidding a suit. For the purposes of bidding, no-trumps rank highest of all, higher even than spades, so we must add some extra rungs to our ladder. 1NT comes in between one spade and two clubs, and 7NT is now the highest possible bid.

This means that the bidding could start:

West	North	East	South
			1♣
1♦	1♥	1♠	1NT etc.

or even:

West	North	East	South
			Pass
Pass	Pass	1♣	Pass
Pass	1♦	Pass	Pass
1♥	Pass	Pass	1♠
Pass	Pass	1NT	Pass etc.

Do you see what we meant when we said that the selection of a trump suit was a sophisticated affair? Look, we have had five rounds of bidding already, we are still only at the one level, and the trump suit still has not been determined!

3

The Scoring

It may seem odd that we have to explain the play of the hand before we can discuss the bidding (which comes first when you actually play!) but in the same way it is essential to have some idea of how the game is scored (which comes last when you actually play!) before we can go into more detail about the bidding.

The scoring in bridge has the reputation of being complicated, and so it is. Fortunately it is quite enough to have only a round idea of what is going on in order to play intelligently and enjoyably. The finer points can always be looked up in the scoring table.

The object of the game is to win the *rubber* which goes to the side first scoring two *games*. In that way it is like a best-of-three sets in a tennis match—if you make two games it is all over; if you reach one game all a decider has to be played.

A game is made by bidding and making a contract (or contracts) that score at least 100 points for your side. Clubs and diamonds—the 'minor' suits—score 20 points for each one bid and made. So bidding and making a contract of three clubs (nine tricks) would score you 3 times 20 equals 60 points. To achieve a game on one hand with a minor suit as trumps you would need to both bid and make five diamonds or five clubs (eleven tricks) for 5 times 20 equals 100 points.

Spades and hearts—the 'major' suits—score 30 points for each one bid and made. So bidding and making a contract of four spades or four hearts yields 4 times 30 equals 120 points—enough for game. It is important to note that you do not carry the extra 20 points that you have earned forward to start you off on the next game.

The scoring in *no-trumps*—the final possibility—is slightly odd, but you soon get used to it! *A contract of 1NT, bid and made, gives you 40 points but all subsequent tricks are worth only 30 points.* The sig-

nificant factor is that a successful contract of 3NT yields 40 plus 30 plus 30 equals 100 points—game with only nine tricks!

It does not help your score if you bid to a contract but fail to make enough tricks. Your side scores nothing at all and your opponents collect penalty points. Equally, making enough tricks for game does not help you very much if you have failed to bid it. You get something for the *over-tricks* but not nearly enough to compensate you for the missed game. Ideally, you only want to bid games that you will make and stop in a *part-score* when you are not able to make enough tricks for game. Admittedly, this is a policy of perfection! *The key thing to remember is that it is only contracts that you bid and make that contribute towards the 100 points you need for game.* It is true that there are a variety of other ways of adding to your overall score but they contribute nothing towards making a game. These points are only added in to your score at the end of the rubber. This is why there are two separate places on the scoresheet for you to enter the points gained by your side—*above the line* and *below the line*.

It is normal for all four players to keep score, so a scoresheet looks like this:

WE	THEY

In the left-hand column (*WE*) you record your successes; in the right-hand column (*THEY*) you write down the points scored by the opposition. Below the line is where the vital points, counting towards game, are entered; above the line go all the bits and pieces, useful nevertheless.

This would be a typical rubber, consisting in this case of five deals:

i) You play in two spades and make nine tricks. This gives you 60 points below the line and 30 above for the overtrick—the extra trick that you made but did not bid.

ii) Your opponents play in four diamonds and make twelve tricks. They score 80 below and 40 above. (You wonder why they did not bid five diamonds—then they would have made a game.)

iii) You play in 1NT and make seven tricks, giving you 40 points below the line. Your assets here now total 100 points so you have made a game. *You celebrate this by drawing a line across BOTH columns*, chopping off the 80 points that your opponents scored on the previous hand. Just like tennis again—if you win the first set by six games to four, your opponents do not carry their four games forward to give them a good start in the next set! Now neither side has a part-score.

iv) Your opponents play in four spades and fall short of their target when they make only nine tricks. They score nothing at all and you collect something above the line. *At this stage it is 50 points for each trick by which they fail, whether they are playing in spades, hearts, diamonds, clubs or no-trumps.*

v) You bid four hearts and make eleven tricks (one overtrick). You score 120 below the line, draw a line across, and also collect 30 points above the line. Furthermore, you have just won the rubber by two games to nil and for this you are rewarded with *a bonus of 700 points*. At last you can see how profitable it is to bid and make games. *(If you had won the rubber by two games to one, your bonus would have been only 500 points.)*

The scoresheet should now look like this:

WE	THEY
(5) 700	
(5) 30	
(4) 50	
(1) 30	40 (2)
(1) 60	80 (2)
(3) 40	
(5) 120	

and it is time to add up. No matter now whether the points are above or below the line; while you played your side scored 1030 points and your opponents 120. The difference is 910 points and, if you had arranged to play for a penny a hundred, you would triumphantly collect 9p from one opponent and your partner 9p from the other. That would be your reward for about half an hour's hard work!

(You round the difference in scores to the nearest 100 so, if you were playing for £1 a hundred, you would only collect £9 and not £9.10.)

There are other ways to score points. You remember that you collected 50 points when your opponents failed to make their contract by one trick? If they had already made a game (when they would be said to be *vulnerable*) *you would have collected 100 points instead of just 50 for every trick by which they fell short of their target.*

Another pleasing possibility is that of *doubling* your opponents. If they bid their way to a contract that you think they cannot make, you can make the bid of *Double* when it is your turn to speak. Effectively this doubles the stakes—you collect far more points if, as you suspected, they cannot make their contract. It is a double-edged weapon however—should they make their contract they will be scoring extra points. This can be expensive for you. Suppose your opponents stop in two hearts (where they would have scored 60 below the line if successful) but you decide to double them. You certainly collect an increased penalty if they go off but should they make their contract they will score twice as many points (60 times 2 = 120) below the line, giving them a game instead of just a part-score.

Furthermore, if you or your partner have been doubled then, when it is your turn to bid, you can say *Redouble*. This doubles the already doubled stakes again. So if you played in one heart redoubled and made your seven tricks you would actually make game with 120 points below the line!

There it all ends—no further doubling of the stakes is permitted. It is important to remember that a subsequent bid by any player (other than Pass) automatically cancels the double or (redouble). So if the bidding has gone:

West	North	East	South
			1♥
Pass	1♠	2♣	Double
Redouble	Pass	2♦	Pass
Pass	Pass		

although East's call of two clubs was doubled (and redoubled!) his subsequent bid of two diamonds was not doubled and the contract is perfectly normal as far as the scoring is concerned.

Apart from one or two other trimmings there is one more important possible source of points. Should a partnership bid and make a contract at the Six level (twelve tricks—*a small slam*) they earn themselves a substantial bonus—*500 points if they are not vulnerable, and 750 points if they have already made a game.* Finally, to bid and make a contract at the Seven level (all thirteen tricks—*a grand slam)* earns a partnership *1000 points if they are not vulnerable* and a magnificent *1500 if they have already made a game*—a spectacular way of winning the rubber!

4

Opening the Bidding

So far all that we have suggested is that a player with a 'fair ration of high cards' will open the bidding, but if he has a poor hand he will say No Bid. That is, at best, pretty vague advice and it is universally accepted that there should be a simple way of assessing the strength of a hand. By far and away the most popular approach is the *point count*. A hand is valued on the following scale:

For every ace	4 points
For every king	3 points
For every queen	2 points
For every jack	1 point

So a hand such as:

♠ AQ74	6 points
♥ AK7	7 points
♦ J4	1 point
♣ K962	3 points
adds up to	17 points

As you can see, in a pack of cards each suit contains 10 points (4+3+2+1) and as there are four suits there are *40 points in the pack*. As there are four players, an average hand contains 10 points. Should you hold only an average hand there is no real reason to expect that your side can make more tricks than the opponents and so a sensible guideline is that you need a little better than average to open the bidding—*perhaps 12 points although some conservative players insist on 13.*

We must stress that point count is only a guideline. Compare these two hands:

	(a)		(b)
	♠ 2		♠ K42
	♥ AK10974		♥ A653
	♦ KJ1083		♦ A65
	♣ 5		♣ J74

(a) has only 11 points in high cards but (b) has 12—yet which hand has the higher trick-taking potential? It is (a) which will be far better than (b) if one of its long suits becomes trumps.

A practical and simple way to adjust the point count in order to allow for distribution is to argue that there is nothing very special about a four-card suit but that for a five-card suit you should mentally add an extra point, and for a six-card suit 2 extra points. So hand (a), which started life with only 11 high-card points, gains 2 more from the heart suit and one more from the diamonds. The adjusted total becomes 14 and the hand is a comfortable opening bid. Hand (b), by contrast, has no long suits and remains, at best, a borderline opening.

Do not take this idea of augmenting the point count too far—if you have been dealt all thirteen spades you do not really care how many points this represents!

This has solved one of the main problems about opening the bidding—when you should do so and when you should pass. The other important decision that you have to make is which suit to bid. Superficially this seems easy, but suppose that you have been dealt a hand like:

	♠ AKQ
	♥ Q52
	♦ J9753
	♣ K2

It is very tempting to bid one spade rather than one diamond, arguing that your spades are very much stronger than your diamonds. Very tempting but very wrong! Consider, if the spades are trumps you will certainly make three tricks, but it is unlikely that your little diamonds will contribute anything. But it is quite possible that you have two more diamonds in your hand than anyone else at the table. This means that if diamonds are trumps your suit will produce at least two tricks—and the top spades are always likely to be tricks whatever trumps are.

The guiding principle, to which there are very few exceptions, is that if you have enough points you should open the bidding with your *longest* suit—the one that contains the most cards—rather than your strongest suit.

An important corollary to this is that, if you are always going to bid your longest suit first, an opening bid always promises at least four cards in the suit named. You may wonder whether this means opening one spade with, perhaps:

♠ 5432
♥ AQ5
♦ J93
♣ AK4

where, although spades is your longest suit, you may feel diffident about suggesting it as trumps. Very soon, when we discuss opening the bidding with 1NT, you will realise that there is a way round this difficulty.

Even with this limited advice you are now in a position to make a sensible bid every time you have the opportunity of opening—pass with 11 or less points (allowing for distribution), bid one of your longest suit with 12 or more.

There are two other possibilities—suggesting that your hand is suitable for no-trumps (dealt with in the next chapter) and opening the bidding with more than one of a suit. We will discuss the higher opening bids, which are not necessarily stronger, later on.

There remains, however, one problem even with a simple opening bid—which suit do you call first if you have two (or even three!) of exactly the same length?

Take the following hand:

♠ AK64
♥ 83
♦ 542
♣ AQ104

You have 13 points, so you want to open the bidding. Suppose you try one spade and your partner has a heart suit that he wants to show you. He has to bid two hearts in order to do so. You are not very keen on his suggestion of hearts as trumps—it is, after all, your shortest suit—and you would like to tell him about your other suit, clubs. But to advance past two hearts you have to bid *three* clubs. Already your side is committed to trying for nine tricks and you have not necessarily found a suit that you both like.

There seems something wrong with this approach so consider the alternative opening bid of one club. As before partner tells you about his hearts but now he can comfortably bid one heart over which you can show your spades by bidding one spade. You have got across just as much information as before (you have an opening bid with a club suit, a spade suit and no great liking for partner's hearts) but you are still at the one level, so far only committed to trying for seven tricks.

It is clear that with two suits of the same length one opening bid works better than the other. In the example above bidding the lower-ranking suit was right but this is not always so. Consider this hand:

♠ 87
♥ AK64
♦ AQ107
♣ 542

First, suppose that you open one diamond. Partner bids one spade and you show your other suit with two hearts. Alternatively, you open one heart and bid two diamonds over the spade response. There seems nothing to choose between the two approaches but, thinking ahead, partner may now want to tell you which of your two suits he prefers. He can pass in both cases if he prefers your second suit, but look what happens if he wants to put you back to the first suit that you bid:

$$1\diamondsuit - 1\spadesuit \qquad \text{or} \qquad 1\heartsuit - 1\spadesuit$$
$$2\heartsuit - 3\diamondsuit \qquad\qquad\qquad 2\diamondsuit - 2\heartsuit$$

Do you see the difference? In the second sequence partner can put you back to your first suit at the two level; in the first he has to do so at the three level.

The following guidelines will lead you to the most practical choice of opening bid nearly all of the time.

i) If you have more cards in one suit than any of the others your problems are solved! Bid it!

ii) If you have two suits of the same length and they are next-door neighbours in the ranking list (spades and hearts, hearts and diamonds, or diamonds and clubs) then you do better to open with one of the higher ranking.

iii) If you have two suits of the same length and they are not next-door neighbours in the ranking list (spades and diamonds, hearts and clubs, or spades and clubs) then you do better to open with one of the lower ranking.

All the hands with two four-card suits are covered by (ii) and (iii) but finally there is the problem of choosing your opening bid when you hold two five-card suits. The simplest approach is to bid the higher ranking when your two suits are touching, and the major suit first when they are not neighbours.

This is not an inflexible rule—for example, with:

♠ K4
♥ 76432
♦ 9
♣ AKQ109

it would be more practical to open one club rather than one heart. If you choose one heart and hear a two-diamond reply, you will have the choice of rebidding your feeble hearts or taking the bidding to the three level (with three clubs) on your minimum opening. By choosing one club instead, you can bid one heart over one diamond, and repeat the strong clubs if the response is one spade. And, if you are dealt five clubs and five spades, open one club. Over a one-diamond or one-heart response you can conveniently rebid one spade, keeping the bidding low, and all your options open.

5

Opening 1NT

As well as opening the bidding with one of a suit there is the possibility of opening 1NT. In principle this suggests a balanced hand (with no long suits and no short suits, such as a singleton or void) and also that you have an all-round hand with no suit that you wish to emphasise. Ideally the bid shows not only evenly distributed cards but also that your high cards are well shared out.

The ideal distribution is 4-3-3-3, but equally acceptable would be 4-4-3-2. Often, though, if the doubleton suit is very weak, a suit opening may work better. So with:

(a)	♠ A105	(b)	♠ J104
	♥ Q963		♥ AKJ3
	♦ A1084		♦ K1092
	♣ K3		♣ 52

1NT is fine with (a) but one heart with (b) looks a little better.

Finally, a 5-3-3-2 hand is also essentially balanced. Now the decision whether to open 1NT or to prefer a suit call depends on the quality of the five-card suit. Consider:

(a)	♠ 108732	(b)	♠ AKJ95
	♥ AQ5		♥ K108
	♦ K108		♦ 75
	♣ A9		♣ Q72

With (a) 1NT is fine, but (b) is a clear-cut one-spade opening. However, if the five-card suit is a minor, you might lean towards opening 1NT.

You may occasionally be tempted by a 5-4-2-2 shaped hand. This is a temptation you should resist. Almost invariably the hand will play better with one of the long suits as trumps.

So, with:

♠ KJ4
♥ Q107
♦ AJ8
♣ Q975

you have no particular reason to stress that you have four clubs and that this is your longest suit. In fact you have the perfect distribution for no-trumps (4-3-3-3) and very little likelihood of making any more tricks if your long suit happens to be trumps. Just consider this example hand—with clubs as trumps it will be a long while before you can take advantage, for you have to follow to three rounds of hearts, spades or diamonds before you can ruff anything. This may seem some something of a negative advantage—suggesting no-trumps—but one of the positive advantages lies in the scoring. *Diamonds and clubs score only 20 points for each one bid and made.* So to achieve a game on one hand you have to bid your way to *five diamonds or five clubs and make no fewer than eleven tricks.* Matters are easier if one of the major suits is trumps. *Spades and hearts score 30 points per trick and you need only to bid to four spades or four hearts (4 x 30 = 120)—only ten tricks—to achieve a game.*

No-trumps offer the best bargain of all although the scoring may strike you as a little strange. The first trick over six in a no-trump contract scores 40 points but after that tricks are worth only 30 points (just as though playing with a major suit as trumps). So playing in a contract of 1NT and taking seven tricks gives our side 40 points; playing in 2NT and taking eight tricks gives you 40 + 30 = 70 points and—wait for it—*playing in 3NT and taking nine tricks gives you 40 + 30 + 30 = 100 points and a game!* So no-trumps represents the easiest route to game (as far as the number of tricks is concerned) but you only want to play in no-trumps if your hands are suitable.

Three examples illustrate the point well.

(a)

West	East
♠ A65	♠ 1072
♥ K83	♥ A94
♦ A72	♦ K93
♣ AKJ5	♣ Q1083

Both players like the idea of clubs as trumps but, equally, both are happy with the idea of no-trumps where there are nine easy tricks available no matter what the opponents lead (A spade, two hearts, two diamonds and four clubs.) Just the same tricks are there if clubs are trumps but no more—there are four inescapable losers (two spades, a heart and a diamond) whatever declarer tries.

(b)

West	East
♠ AKJ5	♠ Q10832
♥ 83	♥ 94
♦ Q107	♦ AK3
♣ A952	♣ K73

This time there are no fewer than ten tricks in sight (five spades, three diamonds and two clubs) but to make game the hands must be played with spades as trumps—in a contract of four spades. In no-trumps there is the very real risk that the opponents will take the first five or six tricks in hearts before you can gain the lead.

(c)

West	East
♠ AQ74	♠ KJ3
♥ 5	♥ 862
♦ AQ1083	♦ KJ9765
♣ 753	♣ 9

33

Now there are only two losers (a heart and a club) if diamonds are trumps, and ten winners in no-trumps. But the opponents can take at least the first ten tricks in hearts and clubs first if you were foolish enough to play in no-trumps.

These examples give a good idea of the hands suitable for play in no-trumps and those which are unsuitable—also the reasons that provide a strong incentive for playing in no-trumps—if your hand and your partner's hand are suitable!

The only angle that we have not discussed is the strength if the hand (in terms of points) required to open 1NT. Clearly it is only the high-card points that count—you cannot add extra points for an exciting distribution if you have a balanced hand!

For reasons that will become very clear when we discuss responding to 1NT in the next chapter, it is extremely important for the opening bid to have quite a narrow range so that partner is put immediately in the picture.

Fashions change—but most of the ranges for the opening bid of 1NT can be classed as *'Weak'* or *'Strong'*. Originally the *weak no-trump* was based on a hand with 13-15 points but nowadays *12-14* is far more popular. In the same way, the *strong no-trump* used to be 16-18 points but now *15-17* is all the rage. You will even find pairs playing a 14-16 no-trump (which is neither fish nor fowl) and a mini no-trump of 10-12 points—which is most definitely on the weak side.

The important thing to note is that they all have a spread of only three points. It would be very nice to open the bidding by saying ''One Weak No-trump'' if you held the right number of points and ''One Strong No-trump'' if your hand was a little stronger, but the rules of the game only allow you to say *''One no-trump''* without qualifications.

When you sit down to play, you arrange with your partner what your opening bid of 1NT shows. Furthermore, this is not a secret that you keep from your opponents. To do so or, indeed, to have any private undisclosed agreements with your partner is strictly illegal and akin to cheating. It is customary, on starting play, to announce to your opponents that you are playing, say, a ''weak no-trump, 12-14 points'' and hear what their arrangements are. Just because North-South play a weak no-trump this does not mean that East-West have to do the same—it is a matter entirely up to the partnership.

It is just as important not to have too many points in your hand when you open 1NT as having too few. So, having arranged to play a weak no-trump (12-14 points) and looking at:

(a) ♠ KJ4	(b) ♠ KJ4	(c) ♠ KJ4
♥ Q105	♥ Q105	♥ KQ5
♦ J85	♦ QJ5	♦ QJ5
♣ A973	♣ A973	♣ A973

—although all the hands are balanced and suitable for no-trumps—you would pass with (a)—too few points to open at all; open 1NT with (b)—perfect in all respects; and open one club with (c)—too many points for 1NT and (as we will see later) far too few points to open 2NT. Remember, *one of a suit shows anything between 12 and 20 points*—with (c) you plan to suggest no-trumps on the next round of bidding.

Should you have arranged to play a strong no-trump (15-17 points), you would still pass with (a); open one club with (b)—too few points to open 1NT but planning to rebid in no-trumps later on; and with (c) you would start with 1NT.

It is also possible to meet players who announce a *'variable no-trump'*. Do not worry, this does not mean that their bid can show anything under the sun, it just means that although they like the idea of the weak no-trump and use it when they are not vulnerable, they are nervous about playing it when vulnerable (when the penalties for failing to make a contract are more severe) and, for safety, switch to playing a strong no-trump. It is a nice idea in theory but—and it happens all too often—players have a tendency to forget the vulnerability!

6

Responding to 1NT

You will remember from the previous chapter that, whether your partnership has agreed to play a weak no-trump or a strong no-trump, you always know (within narrow limits) how many points your partner holds when he opens 1NT.

This is critical and enables the responder to judge whether or not it is a good idea to attempt to bid and make a game. Without worrying you with too much arithmetic, a fair guide is that if the partnership holds *at least 26 points between them* it is worthwhile trying for a game. You do not mind if you reach it with only 25 points, but once you hold only 24 or less points the odds start to tilt against you and you would be better off simply settling for a part-score.

Of course this does not mean that just because you and your partner are the proud joint possessors of, say, 27 points, that making game is certain. You may meet an unfavourable lead or find the missing cards lying badly for you and, as a result, fail to make game. To compensate, every once in a while your partner (never you, of course!) will overbid too optimistically and you will reach a game with insufficient values. You receive a favourable lead, missing cards are well placed for you, and your opponents go wrong in the defence. As a result you register an extremely lucky game. All that you can say is that *25-26 points is about the 'break even' point*. Note that we are talking primarily about balanced hands, suitable for play in no-trumps. Then, and then only, the point count is a good guide. After all, if a player is dealt all thirteen cards in a suit, why should he be interested in the number of points that he holds when he can count thirteen tricks?

Suppose first of all that you and your partner have arranged to play a weak no-trump (12-14 points) and you hear him open 1NT. What action should you take on the following hands?

a) ♠ K87   (b) ♠ K87   (c) ♠ K87   (d) ♠ K87
   ♥ Q105   ♥ Q105   ♥ AK10   ♥ Q105
   ♦ A872   ♦ A872   ♦ AQ82   ♦ A872
   ♣ 972   ♣ AJ9   ♣ J97   ♣ K97

(a) **Pass.** You are very happy with partner's suggestion of no-trumps for, like him, you have a balanced hand. As partner cannot have more than 14 points, your side has a maximum of 23 points between you. Game is extremely unlikely and you can leave partner in what should be a sensible contract whether he is maximum or minimum for the bid.

(b) **3NT.** Again you are happy with no-trumps and, even if partner is minimum for his bid with only 12 points, your side has a combined 26 points. There should be a play for game in no-trumps, so bid it!

(c) **3NT.** Yes, you have got 17 points, but do not get too excited. Your side will almost certainly make ten or eleven tricks but there is nothing whatsoever to be gained from playing in 4NT or 5NT. You still just make game but now there will be a greatly increased chance of something going wrong. It is worth noting that if your hand were even stronger you might essay 6NT or even 7NT. Bidding and making a slam (twelve tricks for a small slam, all thirteen tricks for a grand slam) carries with it a substantial bonus for your side on the scoresheet. *A fair guide is that a combined 33-34 points will offer a fair play for 6NT but you need 37 or more to make the grand slam a good bet.* Remember too that bidding a slam is something of an adventure. While there are attractive bonuses for successes, failure means that you have squandered the opportunity of making an easy game.

(d) **2NT.** With 12 points you do not know whether your side has the combined values for game or not. If partner holds his maximum of 14 points you want to play in 3NT—if he has his minimum of 12 points you want to stop short. The solution is to raise to 2NT, inviting partner to go on with a maximum but warning him to pass with a minimum.

These four example hands have something in common—with each of them you are delighted with partner's suggestion that the hand should be played in no-trumps. Sometimes, however, your hand will be unbalanced with one (or more) long suits and one (or more) short suits. Then your hand will be unsuitable for no-trumps and may well produce extra tricks if your long suit is trumps. Singletons and voids are assets when there is a trump suit but downright liabilities in no-trump contracts.

Take first a hand like this:

♠ 743
♥ J108762
♦ 5
♣ 1093

Your first reaction, with only one point, is to pass anything partner bids. But suppose he opens 1NT? If you leave him there it is most unlikely that your hand will produce any tricks at all for him and the result will be three or four down. Now if only hearts—your long suit—were trumps, your hand would provide some tricks. Remember that partner has a balanced hand and must hold at least two of your hearts. You have probably got three more hearts in your hand than anyone else at the table and if—and only if!—hearts are trumps these will provide three tricks. It is true that to show your hearts you have to bid two hearts, setting a target of eight tricks rather than seven, but if you were offered the choice between going one off in two hearts and watching your partner go three off in 1NT you have an easy decision.

Now the important thing! *A player who replies with two of a suit to 1NT from his partner warns him that he has a bad hand with no interest whatsoever in going any higher.* So if you open 1NT and hear two of a suit from your partner you have no need to take a second look at your hand—you pass automatically. (There is an exception to this which you will find out about when we discuss the Stayman convention in Chapter 18. It will help you to return to this chapter after reading about Stayman.)

The only problem that remains is when you have a good hand (good enough to make game opposite an opening bid of 1NT, that is) which is unbalanced and so unsuitable for play in no-trumps. It would be foolish to go two off in 3NT just because you have enough points if, say, your partnership held eight or nine spades in the combined holding when perhaps you could make an easy game with spades as trumps. The solution is to jump the bidding—one level higher than necessary, suggesting at least a five-card suit and offering partner an alternative to playing in a no-trump game. It is not a royal command. However, this is a bid that invites partner's intelligent co-operation.

So with (a)

West	East
♠ J93	♠ KQ1085
♥ A6	♥ 752
♦ KQ93	♦ J5
♣ K873	♣ AQ2

the bidding goes: 1NT   3 ♠
                4 ♠

But with (b)

West	East
♠ J3	♠ KQ1085
♥ KQ103	♥ 752
♦ A104	♦ J5
♣ K873	♣ AQ2

the bidding goes: 1NT   3 ♠
                3NT

With (a) the opener knows that the partnership holds at least eight spades (and there might be a combined weakness in hearts) so he raises to four spades—the best contract.

With (b) the opener has only two spades and no reason to support his partner. He goes back to 3NT—again the best contract.

Of course if you held six or more cards in your long suit there would be no real reason for enquiring whether the opening 1NT bidder liked the suit—he must hold at least two cards in the suit or else his hand would not be balanced. So if partner opens 1NT, bid a direct four hearts with:

♠ 3
♥ KQ10764
♦ AJ8
♣ QJ5

So far we have only dealt with responding to a weak no-trump (12-14 points). Should you have arranged to play a strong no-trump (say 15-17 points) your responses to 1NT are just as simple. If partner has three more points more for his opening bid, you need three less to push to game.

To summarise, when partner opens 1NT (weak or strong) you have two decisions to make:
(i)   Do I want us to end in game or not?
(ii) Do I like partner's suggestion of playing in no-trumps or not?
In tabular form it looks like this:

	Enough for game	Not enough for game
Happy with NTs	Bid 3NT	Pass
Unhappy with NTs	Bid three of long suit	Bid two of long suit

Yes, there was a halfway house if you were happy enough with no-trumps but not quite sure of game—raising to 2NT—but (for the time being) there is no simple way of inviting, rather than insisting on, game if you are unhappy with no-trumps. The Laws do not allow you to bid two and a half of your longest suit!

7

Responding to One of a Suit

We have dealt with one aspect of responding (replying when partner has opened the bidding) in only one particular case—when partner has opened 1NT. There the problem was relatively straightforward in that (a) partner held a fixed number of points, 12-14, no more and no less, and (b) he held a balanced hand with no long suits and no short suits.

When partner opens with one of a suit, however, you have a very much less accurate picture of his hand. True, you know that he has bid his longest suit (or one of his longest suits if he had a choice) and that he has an opening bid. Counting distribution, though, this may range from 12 points to about 20 points. (With a stronger hand than 20 points he would almost certainly have chosen a more dramatic opening bid.)

Facing one of a suit there are four different courses of action that you can take:

I   Pass
II   **Support partner's suit**
III **Respond in no-trumps**
IV   **Bid a new suit**

I Pass

This is very dull and there is not much to say about it. As partner may have as many as 20 points *it is sensible to find some sort of response whenever you hold 6 or more points and to pass when you have less than 6.* Sometimes this requires a certain amount of will power—for example with:

♠ 1076432
♥ None
♦ J4
♣ 98642

you might be tempted to take action when you hear partner open one heart. Once in a blue moon you will fall on your feet but in real life partner always seems to bid two hearts or even three hearts over your response of one spade. Then, instead of improving matters, you have made them much worse.

II Support partner's suit

The first problem to be considered is "what do you need in partner's suit before you want to support him?". *Generally speaking, you need at least four cards in his suit before you are sure that you have found the best trump suit.* Consider—partner has only guaranteed four cards in the suit that he has named. He may have more but you can only rely on four. Should you raise him, holding only three trumps yourself, this may lead to playing with a combined trump length of only seven cards—which will mean that your opponents hold six. A majority of seven against six is not very satisfactory for you only have to be made to trump twice to leave your opponents with more trumps left than your side, and your reason for choosing that particular suit as trumps will have gone out of the window. The situation changes dramatically should your partnership have started with at least eight cards in the potential trump suit—eight against five—for now, even having been made to ruff twice, your side still has a majority. Should you have only three (or even fewer) cards in partner's suit there will nearly always be a good alternative to supporting him.

Having decided that you want to support partner, the next problem is to determine the level to which you want to raise him. A simple guide, not flawless, but practical enough most of the time, is as follows:

With 6-9 points (and four-card support for partner) raise to the two level (i.e. one spade—two spades). A typical hand for this bid would be:

♠ 10864
♥ 73
♦ AQ5
♣ J962

This, like all other raises of partner's suit, is a *limit* bid, telling him what you have got within narrow limits. It warns him to pass if he has only a minimum or average opening bid but gives him the opportunity to go on to game if he is very strong.

If your hand is a little better (10-12 points, four-card support) you raise him to the three level. So with:

♠ 10864
♥ 73
♦ Q52
♣ AKQ3

a raise of one spade to three spades describes your hand well. There are two points to note about this raise. First, there is little virtue in bidding your clubs—the less that you tell the opponents about your hand the better—for you can only make one suit trumps and your partnership has already found a satisfactory trump suit. And with a good fit in a major suit you have no desire to look for another fit in a minor. Furthermore, if you do bid clubs, your partner will never believe that you hold four of his spades and unnecessary confusion may set in.

Secondly, although your bid is distinctly encouraging, it does not compel partner to bid again. Should he have a minimum opening bid with nothing exciting in the way of distribution he will be well advised to pass.

Should you hold 13-15 points (together with four-card support for partner) you know that, however minimum his opening, between you there are the values for game. So with:

♠ KJ74
♥ 65
♦ AKJ5
♣ Q72

you dare not make any bid that partner can pass short of game and *you should raise one spade directly to four spades.*

(Every once in a while you will hold 16 or more points and be delighted to hear partner open. Whether you like partner's suit or not, you should start your campaign by *jumping one level in a new suit.* So, facing an opening bid of either one heart or one spade with:

♠ KJ74
♥ 65
♦ A63
♣ AKQ4

you should force to game by bidding not just two clubs but three clubs. After this sort of start neither partner is expected to stop bidding until a game has been reached. You can always tell him that you like his suit on the second round of bidding.)

Finally, if partner opens with one of a minor suit, the situation changes slightly. Although raises to the two or three level still have the same meanings, you would be reluctant to raise (say) one diamond to four diamonds. The reason for this is that to make game in a minor you have to win eleven tricks and it is not at all impossible that (even with a good partnership fit in a minor suit) nine tricks in no-trumps will prove an easier game. Suppose partner opens one club with:

> ♠ A76
> ♥ 43
> ♦ A82
> ♣ KQ742

and you hold:

> ♠ K82
> ♥ QJ10
> ♦ K93
> ♣ AJ93

Nine tricks in no-trumps are easy but eleven with clubs as trumps virtually impossible. In response you might bid no-trumps immediately (see the next section of this chapter) or mark time by showing a suit of your own (see the final section of this chapter).

There is one new and important factor to be taken into account when supporting partner's suit. If you had opened one heart with:

> ♠ A6
> ♥ AKJ93
> ♦ 742
> ♣ Q54

which of the following two dummies would you prefer to see?

(a)		(b)	
♠	K54	♠	K542
♥	Q1075	♥	Q1075
♦	1063	♦	3
♣	KJ2	♣	KJ82

They both contain 9 points in high cards but if (a) is your dummy in a heart contract the defenders can take three diamond tricks and the ace of clubs immediately. If (b) is your dummy, however, the defenders can take the ace of clubs and only one diamond trick. Any more diamonds that they lead can be ruffed in dummy (leaving declarer's trump length intact and so providing extra tricks). Hand (b) is therefore more useful than (a) and yet they have identical point counts.

We learnt to adjust the point count of a hand when opening the bidding (when long suits are an asset). Similarly, when supporting partner's suit *and only when supporting partner's suit*, shortages elsewhere are an advantage. A reasonable guide is to add an extra three points for a void, two extra points for a singleton and one for a doubleton.

The adjusted total for hand (b) is therefore $9 + 2 = 11$ points and the hand is worth a raise of one heart to three hearts. Hand (a) has no shortages, so with only nine points it is only worth a raise to two hearts.

It really is important not to confuse the two ways of adjusting the point count that we have met. A void in your hand when you are opening the bidding *may* prove to be an asset but if it is in the suit that partner insists on making trumps it will be a positive liability.

III Respond in no-trumps

A response in no-trumps, just like an opening no-trump bid, suggests a reasonably balanced hand with no suit worth mentioning. The scheme of responses follows closely to that of supporting partner (except that shortages will nor help, nor should you have them!)—you bid the limit of your hand.

With 6-9 points the response is 1NT. So, after hearing one heart from partner, you would bid 1NT with:

♠ K94
♥ 763
♦ QJ9
♣ J973

(You do not want to raise partner's suit with only three trumps; your clubs do not look as though they would set the Thames on fire; and yet you have enough bits and pieces to muster a reply.)

In precisely the same way with 10-12 points and a suitable hand, perhaps:

> ♠ K84
> ♥ 763
> ♦ AKJ
> ♣ J973

you would bid 2NT in reply to one heart. However, with:

> ♠ KQ4
> ♥ 763
> ♦ AKJ
> ♣ J973

your response would be 3NT, showing 13-15 points.

None of these bids insist on partner continuing the bidding—they simply tell him, within narrow limits, what you hold and (as he can *see* his hand) enable him to make a sensible decision as to where the hand should be played. Remember, too, that your response in no-trumps is only a suggestion—not a royal command. You have described your hand accurately but if your partner has a long suit and perhaps a void or singleton he will be well advised to insist on playing with a suit as trumps. He knows that you hold at least two cards in his suit for otherwise your hand would not have been balanced and you would not have put forward the idea of playing in no-trumps.

IV Bid a new suit
Often when your partner opens the bidding you find yourself with neither

support for his suit nor a balanced hand. With enough points to respond (6 or more) all that remains is to tell him about a suit of your own. Your suit, of course, must contain at least four cards for otherwise you would not be suggesting it as a possible trump suit. Generally speaking it is better to show a suit at the one level (if you have one) rather than bid no-trumps immediately for, although partner has bid another suit, he may have four or more cards in your suit. So, with:

♠ Q74
♥ Q1083
♦ K72
♣ J52

although a response of 1NT to one club seems to describe the hand well, it may lead to the wrong contract if partner has, perhaps:

♠ 52
♥ AK72
♦ 83
♣ AQ1094

These two hands will play much better in a heart contract than in no-trumps where the combined weaknesses in spades and diamonds may well prove a handicap.

The important thing to note is that a response in a new suit at the one level does not limit your hand in the same way as do responses in no-trumps or raises in partner's suit. Just because you have 11 points, say, there is no need to jump to two hearts when replying to one diamond.

When you bid a new suit in response to a suit opening from partner you can rely on hearing him make another bid.

It is just as important for the opening bidder to remember this too! If he opens with a suit call and hears a new suit from partner, he *must* make another bid. This is absolutely imperative. It means that you do not have to make wild jumps in the bidding while you and your partner are still discussing the problem of what is your best combined trump suit.

The only exception is when partner has passed initially.

Another factor comes into play when you have to respond at the *two level* in order to show your suit. Over an opening bid of one diamond you are able to bid one heart or one spade to show your suit but it has to be two clubs before that suit can be mentioned.

As you are raising the level of the bidding *and* forcing partner to bid again, it is only reasonable that you should have a little more in high cards than for a response at the one level. *A fair guide is that for a new suit response at the two level you need at least 9 points in high cards and a five-card (or longer) suit.* These are guidelines that can be bent a little way in either respect but not both. So, over one spade from partner, two diamonds would be acceptable with either:

	(a)	or	(b)
♠	74		74
♥	43		AQ72
♦	KQJ976		AKJ3
♣	J93		853

(a) has a good six-card suit to compensate for the shortage of points while (b) with only a four-card suit has plenty of extra points. If, however, you had to respond to one spade with:

	(c)	or	(d)
♠	QJ5		4
♥	4		QJ5
♦	A7632		A7632
♣	9852		9852

you would not be worth two diamonds. You are, nevertheless, too good to pass so one or other of our 'rules' will have to be put temporarily on one side. With (c) the best practical solution is to raise one spade to two spades in spite of having only three-card support. With (d) you do best

49

to respond 1NT in spite of your singleton spade. If partner passes you are likely to be better off in 1NT than one spade; if partner bids any new suit you will certainly have improved matters. Only if he persists with two spades (and he should have a good reason for insisting on spades as trumps!) will you wish that you had passed one spade.

Sometimes there is another way round the problem. Suppose that partner opens one club and you hold:

♠ QJ64
♥ 53
♦ A10872
♣ 94

—easy enough: you bid one diamond. But suppose the opening bid had been one heart? You are not worth two diamonds but at least you have a ready-made alternative in one spade. Do not carry this principle too far. With

♠ QJ64
♥ K3
♦ A10872
♣ J3

you can quite happily bid two diamonds in response to one heart and (as you are well worth a second constructive bid) show your shorter spades on the next round. You only have to distort your hand a little if you are not worth a new suit response at the two level.

A final problem arises when you have two four-card suits in either of which you can respond at the one level. Make the cheaper response. With:

♠ QJ84
♥ K1073
♦ 85
♣ Q92

respond one heart to one diamond or one club. With:

♠ QJ84
♥ 85
♦ K1073
♣ Q92

respond one diamond to one club but one spade to one heart. In this way, if you and your partner have a fit (at least eight cards between you in a suit) it will soon come to light.

Summary

When you respond in no-trumps or raise partner's suit, you do so to the full limit of your hand. When you respond in a new suit there is no hurry. See how it works when you have a hand such as:

♠ QJ84
♥ KQ93
♦ J4
♣ AJ10

If partner opens one diamond or one club, respond one heart. Should partner's next bid be one spade, you go straight to four spades for a fit has been found and as soon as partner had opened the bidding you knew that there were the combined values for game—the problem to start with was that you did not know which game.

Again, partner opens one diamond and, as before, you respond one heart, then hear a bid of two diamonds. Partner could not support your hearts, so he does not have four of them. He has not bid one spade over your one heart so should not have four of them. With no alternative contract (for you have no good fit in any suit) you now go to no-trumps. And it is 3NT, of course, for now you have to limit your hand and, as soon as partner had opened, you knew that you wanted to end in game.

8

Rebidding

In all of the bidding that we have considered so far, a partnership only knows when it wants to end in game (and which game!) after one of its members has made a limit bid—then their partner can judge the situation accurately. We have met two possible starts to this sort of auction: (i) when the opening bid has been 1NT, describing the hand completely and making it easy for the responder to decide the final resting spot and (ii) when the opening bid has been one of a suit and the responder has made a limit bid, either raising his partner's suit to the two, three, four or five level, or responding on no-trumps at the one, two or three level. In both cases the responder has described his hand both in strength (to within a point or two) and in type (support for partner or balanced).

Much of the time, however, the bidding starts one of a suit, then one of a new suit—for example:

West	North	East	South
			1 ♥
Pass	1 ♠	Pass	?

Here neither South nor North has limited his hand. South may hold anything between 12 and 20 points; he may have a balanced hand (with the wrong number of points to have opened 1NT), he may have a two-suited hand, he may have support for his partner; he may have a one-suited hand. Equally, the potential of the North hand is a complete mystery. All that is known is that he has at least four spades and at least 6 points. He may have as many as 15 points, as with more it is likely that he would have tried something more exciting for his first response.

From this start anything can happen. If only 12 points are facing 6 (less than half the points in the pack) the partnership will have done well if they find a part-score that they can make. Between them, though, they may easily have enough for game or (if the opener has 19-20 points and the responder 14 or 15) a small slam or even a grand slam.

Very often the opener's rebid will go some way towards defining his hand more closely—both as regards what type of hand he holds (balanced, two-suited etc.) and how good his opening bid is (weak, medium or strong).

There are four types of rebid that the opener can make:

I   **Support partner's suit**
II   **Rebid in no-trumps to show a balanced hand**
III **Repeat his own suit with nothing else to show**
IV   **Bid a new suit**

I Support partner's suit

Just as when supporting a suit that partner has opened, *you like to have at least four cards in partner's suit before you support him.* Every so often you 'bend' matters slightly and support him with only three, but that is very much an exception.

Take the following three hands on which you have opened one diamond and heard a response of one heart:

(a)	♠ 64	(b)	♠ K4	(c)	♠ K4
	♥ KQJ2		♥ KQJ2		♥ KQJ2
	♦ AK762		♦ AK762		♦ AK762
	♣ 84		♣ 84		♣ K4

In every case you are delighted to support partner's suit. Do not get too excited by the quality of the support that you have in (a)—*two hearts, suggesting a minimum opening bid (12-15 points)* is quite sufficient. Unless partner is prepared to make a further forward-going bid, you will not miss anything.

With (b) your hand is 3 points stronger and a raise to *three hearts describes the hand well—16-18 points,* good support and distinctly encouraging. Should partner have only a miserable 6 or 7 points, he is quite free to pass.

With (c), no matter how feeble partner may be (remember, he could have passed your opening bid), you are full value for *a raise to four hearts—good support and 19-20 points—*and good enough to have a go at making game even if partner is minimum.

II Rebid in no-trumps

Just like an opening bid of 1NT, a rebid in no-trumps promises a balanced hand. The simplest approach follows the same lines as when you are supporting partner's suit so with the following three hands, after the start of 1♦—1♥, rebid at different levels:

	(a)	♠ KQ4	(b)	♠ KQ4	(c)	♠ KQ4
		♥ 65		♥ A6		♥ A6
		♦ AJ93		♦ AJ93		♦ AJ93
		♣ K1052		♣ K1052		♣ KQ105

(a) **rebids 1NT, suggesting 12-15 points,** and more descriptive than showing the club suit and (by bidding two suits) suggesting a less balanced hand.

(b) **rebids 2NT, suggesting 16-18 points.** Encouraging certainly, but not forcing—partner is free to pass if his response was based on only 6 or 7 points or to retreat to three hearts with a completely minimum hand and a six-card suit. The opener should pass this.

(c) **rebids 3NT, suggesting 19-20 points** and (clearly) insisting on game no matter how weak partner's response.

As you can see, there is a certain overlap between opening 1NT and rebidding 1NT. Some partnerships, by arrangement, open all balanced 12-14 hands with 1NT and bid a suit first, with a view to rebidding 1NT, with 15-16 points. This means that after, say, 1♦—1♥, 2NT now shows

17-18 points rather than 16-18. This alternative approach is slightly more descriptive (and so more accurate) but is not universally adopted.

There is one further problem which arises when partner's initial response has been at the two level (for example, 1♦—2♣). Now the responder has promised at least 9 points instead of the 6 he would have guaranteed had he only bid a new suit at the one level. It is only reasonable to take this into account when rebidding in no-trumps—after all, a rebid of 1NT is no longer available. So—rebid 2NT with 15-16 points, and 3NT with 17-18.

III Rebid your own suit

This is the course of action you adopt with a one-suited hand—you cannot support partner, you have not got a balanced hand, and you have no other suit that you can show conveniently. All that a simple rebid of your own suit shows is a minimum hand, at least five cards in your own suit, and nothing more constructive to say. Consider these two hands:

(a)		(b)	
	♠ A74		♠ A74
	♥ 3		♥ 3
	♦ KQ10983		♦ AKJ1093
	♣ Q85		♣ A85

With hand (a) (after 1♦—1♥), you have nothing further to say than two diamonds. With hand (b), which has extra values but nothing else to show, three diamonds is the most descriptive bid—encouraging, 16-18 points combined with a good six-card suit, but not forcing.

IV Bid a new suit

With all of the preceding types of hand you have been able to limit your hand with your rebid. In other words, having made any one of these rebids, you can lean back in your chair and relax—partner has a fair idea of your hand (both type and strength), can see his own hand and—as a result—is in a good position to make a sensible decision as to where and how high the hand should be played.

When it comes to bidding a new suit, however, the position changes. It would be nice if you could limit your hand as well as tell partner about your second suit but it simply is not practicable. For example, after 1♥—1♠, you might want to show a diamond suit but it would be very awkward if you had to jump to four diamonds in order to show 19-20 points. It could easily be that 3NT might prove to be the best game contract and your bid would have taken you past this. So, normally, when the opener bids a new suit he does not hurry. If, after this start, he rebids two diamonds he might have only 12 points but he might be as strong as 17 or 18. The only exception to this principle is illustrated by a hand like this:

> ♠ K74
> ♥ AKJ85
> ♦ AKJ3
> ♣ 2

You open one heart and hear a response of one spade. You know that your side has the values for game, but which game? It might be four spades, four hearts, five diamonds or even 3NT—you do not know as so much depends on partner's hand. The danger of only bidding two diamonds is that partner, with a minimum and preferring your diamonds to your first suit (hearts) might pass. The solution is to jump to three diamonds. *A jump bid in a new suit, as a rebid, commits both members of the partnership to carry on bidding until a game is reached.* At the moment you have no idea what partner will do over three diamonds but, whatever action he chooses, he cannot pass and you will have more information about his hand before finally choosing in which game you want to play.

Although going a little beyond the scope of this chapter, it is worthwhile giving a little thought to the opener's third bid in the auction—assuming matters go that far! Suppose that you hold:

♠ AKJ74
♥ QJ873
♦ K5
♣ 2

and the bidding starts:

South	North
1 ♠	2 ♦
2 ♥	2NT
?	

With 14 points in high cards you are prepared to go on to game, but which game? Four spades, four hearts or 3NT? You do best to complete the picture of your hand and let partner make the final decision. The correct advance is to bid three hearts. Consider—you have bid hearts twice and must therefore have five, but you bid spades *first*—so you must have at least five spades as well. Now partner can choose.

It is interesting to note that there is no need to rebid your spades in order to show five—bidding your second suit twice conveys even more information.

9

Suit Establishment

The usual problem, when a hand is played, is that neither side has enough tricks. For example, if the contract is 3NT the declarer rarely has in sight the nine tricks that he requires. Equally the defenders rarely have the five immediate winners that they will need to defeat the contract. Aces are always tricks (but neither side ever has enough of them!) and everyone aims to develop extra tricks with lower-ranking cards that are not immediate winners.

Take a simple example where South has become declarer in 3NT, say, after he has opened 1NT and been raised to game by his partner.

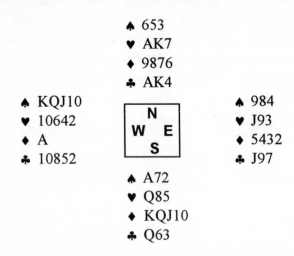

Looking at all four hands it is easy to see that declarer (as soon as he gains the lead) has seven immediate winners (one spade, three hearts and three clubs)—two short of his requirements. The defenders have only one trick instantly available (the ace of diamonds) and would like to come to four more.

Now the play. The first point to make is that it is not in West's best interests to lead his ace of diamonds. If he does so he immediately establishes three tricks in the suit for declarer who will no longer have the slightest trouble in coming to not just nine but ten tricks. West is far better advised to lead his longest and best suit, spades/ He should choose the king for reasons that will become clear later and, if declarer decides not to win the trick at once, persist with the suit until finally South is forced to take his ace. Note the difference—declarer still has only seven tricks in sight but West has established no fewer than three tricks in spades.

It will not help South to play off his winners in hearts and clubs—nothing extra will come in and just look at what happens at the end. When declarer finally leads a diamond West will be in a position to win tricks with his ace of diamonds, any spades that he has left, and the tens of hearts and clubs, totalling no fewer than six tricks for the defence.

Instead, as soon as he decides to win with the ace of spades, declarer must *establish* his diamond suit, leading any of his equally important cards until the ace is taken. As a result West wins with his ace of diamonds and can take the rest of his spades. The defence will have done its best but declarer still makes his contract.

We have used the word *'establish'* and this is a very important concept. Extra tricks in a suit may be established in several ways—as long as you have sufficient material and time!

First take the suit that we have just considered:

♦ 9876

♦ KQJ10

With only the ace missing there is only one trick to be lost while three are established. Of course, all of the high cards do not have to be in one hand:

♦ Q1086

♦ KJ97

would be just as good. Now take:

♦ J32

♦ Q104

Here you have three equally important cards (the queen, the jack and the ten) and your opponents have only two cards (the ace and the king) to beat them. By leading high cards and losing two tricks in the suit you will eventually come to a trick. Note that you have to play high cards—it will do no good leading the four and following with the two from the North hand; the opponents will not waste an ace or a king on that but will simply win cheaply with a much lower card.

Two words of warning—with a suit such as:

♦ J10

♦ Q9

although you have no fewer than four equally important cards and there are only two cards out to beat them, you will not make any progress here for all four of your high cards will fall in two tricks, losing to the ace and king. And again, with:

♦ J32

♦ Q54

you cannot be sure of a trick. Your jack could lose to the king, your queen to the ace, and you will have nothing left.

On the brighter side:

♦ 432

♦ J1098

is worth a potential trick for after losing to the queen, king and ace you will have a winner left. The only question with a suit like this is whether you will have the necessary time or not. Remember that you have to lead the suit no fewer than four times before you eventually come to a trick.

It is not just high cards that can be established—low cards can play their part too, provided that you have enough of them. You have no trouble in estimating your total of winners with a suit of:

♦ 543

♦ AKQ

but suppose that you had another low card in your hand? Say:

♦ 543

♦ AKQ2

Is there any prospect of anything extra? (Before answering, let us for the moment dismiss any worries about our winners or potential winners being trumped by an opponent. So far we are just considering a single suit by itself. Imagine that you are playing in no-trumps or that we are looking at the trump suit itself.) Now, back to our suit. There are still the three obvious winners but anything extra depends on how evenly the missing cards are divided between West and East. Time for some arithmetic, but nothing too taxing. Your side holds seven cards in the suit, leaving six for your opponents. You must hope that they hold three each—perhaps:

♦ 543

♦ J97   ♦ 1086

♦ AKQ2

Then, after cashing your top cards, your little two becomes a winner. Finding the favourable 3-3 break is about a one in three chance (36% to be precise) so this is only a possible extra trick, by no means to be relied upon as a certainty.

There are many suits like this—consider:

♦ 6543

♦ AKQ2

Our familiar three top tricks, but now there are only five cards missing and all you need is for either opponent to hold three of them and his partner two—about two chances in three (68%).

And if you went even further with:

♦ 76543

♦ AKQ2

you will make all five tricks unless you are unlucky enough to find one opponent holding all four missing cards.

It is instructive to think of

♦ 43

♦ AKQ2

Now, unless an opponent obligingly discards a card in this suit, you have no chance at all of coming to anything extra for there are no fewer than seven cards missing and either East or West must hold at least four of them.

There is a very simple rule of thumb here—if your side holds more cards in a suit than the opponents, you may make something extra with your low cards; if your side holds fewer cards than your opponents, you have very little chance of your low cards working for you.

Consider another complete deal:

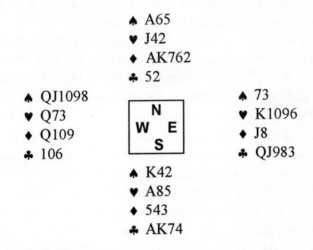

♠ A65
♥ J42
♦ AK762
♣ 52

♠ QJ1098
♥ Q73
♦ Q109
♣ 106

♠ 73
♥ K1096
♦ J8
♣ QJ983

♠ K42
♥ A85
♦ 543
♣ AK74

Again, to avoid the possible complications of a trump suit, we will suppose that South is playing in 3NT after he has opened 1NT and been raised to game. (Note that North did not bother to show his diamonds. Facing what he knows to be a balanced hand of 12-14 points, the eleven tricks needed for game with diamonds as trumps would be far too ambitious, but the nine required for game in no-trumps a much more reasonable target.)

West led the queen of spades—with no immediate winners in his hand he hoped to establish tricks in his long suit. South inspected dummy and could see only seven top tricks (two spades, one heart, two diamonds and two clubs). Nothing extra would come in from the spades, hearts or clubs for in all these suits the defenders held more cards than declarer and dummy together. That left the diamonds, a suit in which five cards were missing, and offering no fewer than two extra tricks if these missing cards broke 3-2. What could be simpler?

Hold on a minute! There are one or two traps in the order in which the cards have to be played to ensure success, even if the diamonds do behave.

First of all, a decision has to be made as to whether to win the first trick with the ace or king of spades (or even to let the queen win!). Secondly, a trick must be lost in the diamond suit before the two extra tricks can be enjoyed. If South begins by cashing everything in sight before giving up a diamond the defenders will take the rest of the tricks. Try again. Win the opening lead with dummy's ace and play off the ace, king and another diamond. This is better—the diamonds are established while declarer is still in control of the other three suits. But now there is a new problem—there are indeed two winning diamonds in dummy but no remaining way of getting the lead there (short of hiring a helicopter!)

There were two ways round this problem. Declarer could have been careful to win the opening spade lead with his king in hand, keeping the ace in dummy as an entry to the soon-to-be-established diamonds. Alternatively, if he had made the mistake of winning the spade lead in the wrong hand, declarer could still recover by letting an opponent win either the first or second round of diamonds. If a trick has to be lost in a suit sooner or later, it frequently pays to lose it sooner. This goes against the grain with many beginners who are unnecessarily reluctant to lose the lead at any time if it can possibly be avoided. Often it is absolutely necessary—suppose that the contract is the same but the ace of spades has been transferred to the South hand so that the deal becomes:

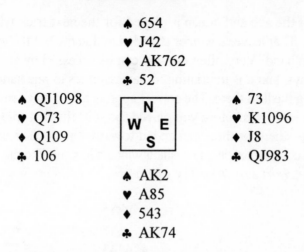

As before West leads a spade and declarer can only win this in his own hand. Unless he gives up an early diamond, leaving:

	♦ AK76	
♦ Q10		♦ J
	♦ 54	

in the suit, with four tricks established and ready to run next time declarer gains the lead, he will end with seven tricks rather than nine.

While on the subject of traps in the play, there is another way for declarer to deprive himself of his heritage. Suppose that dummy and he have a suit of:

♦ AQ2

♦ K3

and all that he wants to do is cash the three tricks that obviously belong to him. Starting with the lead in his own hand, there is a right way to go about it and a wrong way. If the first lead is the three, it does not matter

65

which of the ace and queen is played for the next trick will be won by the king. That leaves a winner stranded in dummy but the lead in declarer's own hand. Very often dummy can be accessed by another suit but not always, and it is infuriating to have winners in one hand but no way of getting the lead there. The correct approach is to make sure that (wherever the lead was before you played the suit) the first trick is won with the king—then the three can be led towards the queen and ace.

The secret, when simply cashing winners in a suit like this is *high cards from the short suit first*. Try one more:

◆ KQ2

◆ AJ43

All four top cards in the suit but here dummy is the 'short' hand—only three cards in the suit compared with declarer's four. So, following the rule, the first two tricks should be won with the king and queen—then nothing can go wrong. To muddle the play of such a suit and leave winners stranded is said to be *blocking* the suit—and this is not a good thing. Sometimes, of course, a suit is blocked for you when it is dealt—for example:

◆ KQJ2

◆ A

Four winners but the ace blocks the suit. Usually it will be right to cash the ace early in the play and hope that you will be able to get the lead to dummy with the aid of another suit.

10

Finessing

There is another extremely important way in which extra tricks may be generated. First, consider two suit combinations which are beautifully simple:

(a)   ♥ AK   (b)   ♥ KQ

      ♥ 32   ♥ 32

With (a) there are two tricks no matter where you start with the lead. With (b) there is one potential trick, again irrespective of where you start with the lead and no matter which opponent holds the missing ace.

But what about:

(c)   ♥ AQ

      ♥ 32

There is only one obvious trick, the ace, and the problem lies in trying to make a trick with the queen as well. There is no point in simply leading the ace for the chances of the king falling singleton are almost zero. Equally, it will not help to lead the queen for whichever opponent holds the king will simply win the trick. In other words, it cannot help you to lead the suit from the North hand (whether it is declarer or dummy). Instead, arrange (via another suit if necessary) for the lead to be in the South hand and lead low towards the ace-queen, You must hope that it is West, rather than East, who holds the all-important missing king. Then, when West plays low on the lead (it will never help him to play the king if he has got it) you try the effect of the queen. If the cards lie favourably East will be unable to beat this and you will have two tricks in the suit.

And if East has the king all the time? Well, he will win your queen with it and you will be restricted to only one trick. Of course as declarer you cannot see your opponents' cards. When you start to play the suit you have no idea who holds the missing king. But by playing as suggested you give yourself a 50% chance of an extra trick, while any other play gives you no chance of making more than the ace.

This manoeuvre is known as *taking a finesse*. Half the time it will win, half the time it will lose but you have lost nothing by trying it and may gain that vital extra trick.

There are countless examples of *finessing—attempting to win a trick with a lower card by hoping that a higher card (held by an opponent) is well placed for you.* Here are just a few, some with extra nuances to look out for.

♥ AQJ

♥ 432

You must, as before, hope that West has the king. You must get the lead into the South hand before tackling the suit. Then, if the finesse of the queen (or the jack—it does not matter) succeeds, you must get the lead back to South before touching the suit again and repeating the finesse.

                    ♥ AQJ10
    ♥ K765   ♥ 98
                    ♥ 432

Here you have the opportunity to take the finesse no fewer than three times. It is worth noting that West should not despair—appreciating that his king is badly placed he might be tempted to play it in a fit of pique. He should realise that South has to get the lead into his own hand no fewer

68

than three times in order to come to four tricks in the suit. And he may not have three entries to hand, in which case West will eventually score with his king.

♥ AQ10

♥ 432

This suit offers scope for a *double finesse*. First a finesse of the ten followed, later in the play, by a finesse of the queen will give you three tricks if you are lucky enough to find West with both the king and the jack. If he holds just one of these missing honours and not the other, one finesse will work and the other one will fail resulting in just two tricks for declarer. And if East turns up with both the king and the jack both finesses will fail leaving declarer with just the one trick (the ace) with which he started and the consolation that, no matter how he had played the suit, he could not have done better.

♥ QJ10

♥ A32

Here you can always make two tricks by brute force but you can make three if you find East with the king. It does no good leading the suit from the South hand for, whichever defender holds the missing king, a trick will be lost. But if the suit is tackled by leading an honour from the North hand and letting it run round (unless East plays the king), repeating the manoeuvre on the next trick, you will make three tricks in the suit whenever East started with the king. And if West holds the king there is nothing to be done however the suit is played. Remember, finesses win half the time and lose half the time but if you do not try them you will not make any extra tricks.

♥ K4

♥ 32

This is perhaps the simplest possible suit combination where you may or may not take a trick with your high card. One thing is certain; leading the suit from the North hand will not help. Leading the king is doomed to failure and leading the four loses to something small and leaves the king to fall under the ace later in the play. Now try leading low from the South hand towards the king. Half the time West will have started with the ace and, if he plays it, the king will score later. If West follows low to the first lead, you try the king—successfully if the ace was well-placed for you. You have to learn to smile philosophically when East turns up with the ace!

The secret of this last suit, as with so many finesses, lies in *leading from the hand that contains nothing of value towards the hand that has something of value*. In that way one of the opponents has to commit himself to playing a card before you decide what to play from the 'something'.

Again:

♥ KQ3

♥ 542

One trick for certain but you can take advantage of West holding the ace to make two, provided that you can get the lead twice into the South hand.

<pre>
          ♥ KQJ3
♥ A1098   ♥ 76
          ♥ 542
</pre>

Here you have only two tricks to come if the suit is led from the North

70

hand, but three if you can arrange to lead 'from nothing towards something' three times.

Try assessing your prospects with this suit:

♥ KQ654

♥ 32

assuming that you have plenty of entries to both hands and plenty of time to develop your suit. One trick, two tricks or more? Well, everything will depend on (1) which defender holds the ace and (2) how evenly the suit divides—yes, as we discussed earlier, your low cards may play their part.

This would be the least favourable setup:

♥ KQ654

♥ 7   ♥ AJ1098

♥ 32

when, whatever you tried, you could only make one trick. At the other end of he scale, the missing cards might lie like this:

♥ KQ654

♥ A108   ♥ J97

♥ 32

You have got the idea now—lead towards the North hand. Say the king wins—come back to hand with another suit and lead low again. Say the queen wins—now all that remains to do is to lead a third round of the suit (on which your opponents' ace and jack fall together) and you will have two more tricks to come from North's low cards.

Consider this suit combination:

♥ Q32

♥ A54

This is a slightly confusing suit. It looks like a finesse—lead the queen and hope that East has the king?—but this can never work. If West has the king he will win, while if East has the king he will play it on your queen. After winning your one trick with the ace you will have nothing left. Instead, try leading low from the South hand towards the queen. Then every time West holds the king there will be two tricks for you, while if East holds the king there was nothing to be done.

Another important suit combination is illustrated by:

♥ AJ10

♥ 432

Here there is one certain trick but good prospects of a second. The plan, as usual, is to lead low towards the high cards in the North hand. Should West play either of the missing honours your problems are solved. More likely, West follows with a low card and you finesse the ten (or jack). Should this lose to East, you wait until South has the lead again and this time finesse the jack (or ten, whichever is left). It is easy to assess your chances. Whenever West has both the king and queen, or either, you will make two tricks. Only on your unlucky days when you find East with both missing honours will you be restricted to one trick.

Finally a little curiosity:

♥ AJ2

♥ K103

Two obvious tricks (the ace and king) and a possible third. Can you always make a third trick? Yes, provided that you can guess which opponent holds the missing queen! If you think that it is West, lead low from the South hand and (when West plays low) finesse the jack. If instead you think that East holds the queen, lead low from the North hand and finesse the ten. Three tricks guaranteed, as long as you are clairvoyant! To be fair, sometimes the opponents' bidding may have given you a clue. For example, if East bids something and his partner remains silent, East is far more likely to hold any missing high cards than his partner.

11

Trumps

So far everything that we have said about building up extra tricks applies equally to the play in no-trump contracts and when there is a trump suit. The introduction of a trump suit, however, adds a new dimension to the play of the cards. Generally this will be of the advantage of the declarer—after all, he and his partner have chosen the trump suit and will presumably hold more cards in it than the opponents. Every so often, however, something nasty will happen—one of your aces may get trumped, and that is something that will never happen to you in a no-trump contract.

The important question is: *How can a trump suit be used to develop extra tricks for declarer?* If you think of a suit all by itself, perhaps:

♠ 987

♠ AKQJ10

it is easy to see that it is worth five tricks whether it is trumps or not. Suppose that it is the trump suit (spades, say) and introduce another suit:

♠ 987
♥ 432

♠ AKQJ10
♥ 5

Your opponents lead hearts and you trump the second round. You have made a trick but you only have four left—in other words you have ended up with the same number of tricks with which you started. And yet there

74

is something curiously satisfying about trumping something, especially if it is an opponent's ace or king. Having trumped one heart—which you had to do or else lose the trick—there is an almost irresistible temptation to get the lead into dummy (with a diamond or a club) and ruff another heart. Two tricks in the bag from your trump suit but only three more to come—you still make just five tricks from the suit. There is another built-in danger, too. When you finally get round to drawing trumps you may find an opponent with four spades—little ones, maybe, but if he has one more than you have left he will eventually make an undeserved trick.

Now make a slight change in the heart suit:

♠ 987
♥ 5

♠ AKQJ10
♥ 432

Again the opponents lead hearts against your spade contract. Seeing only one in dummy it is likely that they will switch to something else for the second trick. When you first gain the lead in the South hand you will be able to ruff a heart in dummy—a trick from your trump suit and you still have your original five winners in hand. In other words, an extra trick. Indeed, by trumping your last heart on the table you end with another extra trick and the conclusion that:

Trumping in the short trump hand (usually dummy) and leaving the length in the long trump hand (usually declarer) undisturbed brings in extra tricks; trumping in the long trump hand does not.

Like so many guidelines and axioms, this is a good principle to follow but—inevitably—you will come across exceptions.

The last example illustrates well the value of a shortage in a side suit—if the suits had been:

♠ 987
♥ None

♠ AKQJ10
♥ 432

with a void in dummy instead of a singleton, then, if nobody led trumps and declarer could get the lead into his own hand three times, three ruffs in dummy would mean that declarer came to no fewer than eight tricks from his trump suit.

Even a doubleton, though not as immediate as a void or a singleton, can be the source of a potential trick.

♠ 987
♥ 65

♠ AKQJ10
♥ 432

You are bound to lose two tricks in the heart suit sooner or later but if you go out of your way to lose them quickly—leading the suit yourself if necessary—while dummy still has at least one trump left, you will be able to ruff your last heart on the table for an extra trick. It is worth noting that if you start off by drawing all of your opponents' trumps at least three rounds of the suit will be necessary. This will leave dummy with no trumps at all and the defenders, when they get in, will be able to take three heart tricks and not two.

It all leads to another golden rule:

Draw trumps unless there is a good reason not to.

Next, a couple of complete deals to illustrate this idea.

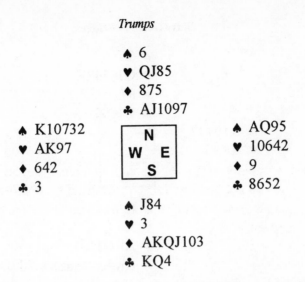

```
                    ♠ 6
                    ♥ QJ85
                    ♦ 875
                    ♣ AJ1097
    ♠ K10732      ┌─────────┐      ♠ AQ95
    ♥ AK97        │    N    │      ♥ 10642
    ♦ 642         │ W     E │      ♦ 9
    ♣ 3           │    S    │      ♣ 8652
                  └─────────┘
                    ♠ J84
                    ♥ 3
                    ♦ AKQJ103
                    ♣ KQ4
```

Suppose that as South you and your partner bid to five diamonds and West leads the ace of hearts. After looking in dummy he switches to the three of clubs and you win in your hand (your hand, to avoid blocking the suit). Is this a hand where you want to draw trumps immediately (which may remove all of dummy's trumps at the same time) or do you need to try to utilise dummy's singleton spade before tacking trumps?

First of all, count your winners if you do draw trumps. Six diamonds and five clubs give you the eleven tricks that are all you need for your contract and you should lose no time in drawing trumps, enjoying your club winners and claiming your contract. If you had not counted your winners and decided it was a hand for ruffing spades in dummy, what would have happened? Say that after winning the club you had given up a spade, preparatory to ruffing a losing spade or two on the table. East would win and return his partner's lead of a club. West would ruff and that would be three tricks for the defence and defeat for five diamonds.

Now change the scene a little and make the deal look like this:

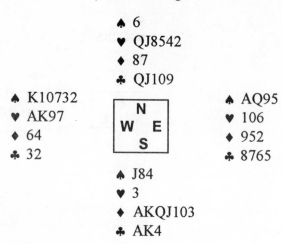

♠ 6
♥ QJ8542
♦ 87
♣ QJ109

♠ K10732   ♠ AQ95
♥ AK97   ♥ 106
♦ 64   ♦ 952
♣ 32   ♣ 8765

♠ J84
♥ 3
♦ AKQJ103
♣ AK4

Again you are in five diamonds and again West cashes the ace of hearts before switching to the three of clubs. Just as before you count your winners and find that now there are only ten (six diamonds and four clubs) and that simply drawing trumps will leave you a trick short. Dummy's heart suit cannot be used and the only possibility of an eleventh trick lies in being able to ruff a spade safely in dummy. After winning the club in hand, you must give up a spade immediately. If West had (as on the previous deal) started with a singleton club, too bad; you will go down when he scores his ruff but there was nothing that you could have done about it. As the cards lie, no-one trumps a club and you can ruff a spade safely on the table to give you your eleventh trick. Note that you could not afford to play even one round of trumps before conceding a spade—the opponents will be quick to win the spade and lead another trump, drawing dummy's last tooth before you were able to use it.

So far we have met two distinct ways of going about the play in a suit contract—drawing trumps and cashing winners; and putting off drawing trumps until you have taken one or more ruffs in the short trump hand. Perhaps a deal like the following represents a halfway house between the two approaches:

♠ 4
♥ KJ874
♦ AKQ
♣ K874

♠ Q65
♥ AQ1093
♦ J53
♣ A6

As South you have ended in six hearts and West leads the two of diamonds. A count of immediate winners gives ten (five hearts, three diamonds, and two clubs) and two extra tricks are required to make the small slam. Ruffing two spades in dummy will yield these tricks but that does not necessarily mean that you should lead a spade at the second trick for, if the diamond lead happened to be a singleton, you would risk going down—quite unnecessarily! As there are only three trumps missing, there can be no possible objection to drawing these first, taking three rounds of the suit if necessary. Then you can give up a spade with a clear conscience. The defenders can no longer ruff anything. Remember: *"Draw trumps unless there is a good reason not to."* Here there was no good reason not to.

There is a third, quite different idea for generating tricks with the aid of a trump suit. Not drawing trumps, not deferring drawing trumps, but never drawing trumps! It sounds a dangerous game but consider this deal:

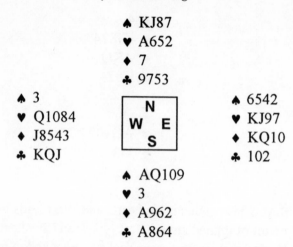

♠ KJ87
♥ A652
♦ 7
♣ 9753

♠ 3
♥ Q1084
♦ J8543
♣ KQJ

♠ 6542
♥ KJ97
♦ KQ10
♣ 102

♠ AQ109
♥ 3
♦ A962
♣ A864

Suppose that as South you have reached four spades (perhaps, optimistically, by bidding 1♦—1♥—1♠—3♠—4♠) and get the lead of the king of clubs. First, you count certain winners and the result is not good!—four spades and three outside aces only gives seven. Secondly, could you ruff some of your losing diamonds in dummy? It all starts smoothly enough (win with ace of clubs, cash the ace of diamonds, ruff a diamond in dummy) but the only way back to the South hand will be by using up trumps. Does that give the vital clue? Yes; after starting as suggested, play off the ace of hearts and ruff a heart in hand. The next four tricks consist of diamond ruff, heart ruff, diamond ruff and a heart ruff. At the end of which you will have nine tricks in the bag and still hold the ace and king of trumps. There is no way to make them separately but who cares? You have made your contract. This is called playing a *cross-ruff*—you make as many of your trumps as possible, separately, and never draw the opponents'. At the end East has nothing but trumps left and is reduced to ruffing his partner's winners!

Nobody rings a bell when it is time to play a hand on a cross-ruff but here are some of the clues to look out for and help you recognise the right type of hand. Insufficient tricks if you draw trumps, plenty of trumps in both hands. A suit facing a shortage and a shortage facing a suit. These features were all present in our example.

Another important possibility in suit play is the possibility of establishing a side suit with the aid of your trumps. The suit to be established can either be in declarer's hand or in dummy, as illustrated by the following examples:

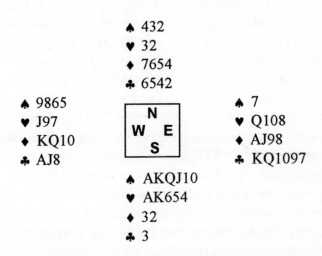

```
                    ♠ 432
                    ♥ 32
                    ♦ 7654
                    ♣ 6542
   ♠ 9865                          ♠ 7
   ♥ J97          N                ♥ Q108
   ♦ KQ10      W     E             ♦ AJ98
   ♣ AJ8          S                ♣ KQ1097
                    ♠ AKQJ10
                    ♥ AK654
                    ♦ 32
                    ♣ 3
```

Suppose that you are declarer with the South hand in a spade contract and the defenders start with three rounds of diamonds. You ruff the third. If you draw trumps you will end with exactly seven tricks. There is no possibility of ruffing all three of your losing hearts in dummy—someone is sure to play a higher trump than dummy very soon—but look what happens if you play off the ace and king of hearts and ruff just one heart on the table? You are in luck, for all six of the missing hearts have fallen in three rounds and you are left with two extra winners in the suit. Now there is no reason not to draw trumps and, after enjoying your established heart winners, you end with no fewer than ten tricks.

This next deal has a similar theme and also introduces a new sort of finesse—one that depends upon the assistance of a trump suit.

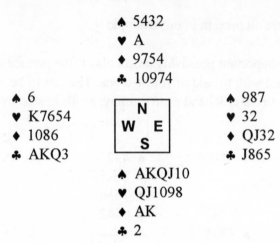

```
              ♠ 5432
              ♥ A
              ♦ 9754
              ♣ 10974
♠ 6                              ♠ 987
♥ K7654          N               ♥ 32
♦ 1086        W     E            ♦ QJ32
♣ AKQ3           S               ♣ J865
              ♠ AKQJ10
              ♥ QJ1098
              ♦ AK
              ♣ 2
```

Imagine that South has ended in six spades (he and his partner are aggressive bidders!) and West starts with the ace and king of clubs, South ruffing the second. The king of hearts is missing and the prospects of trumping three or four hearts in dummy without either of the defenders being able to score with a trump slightly higher than any of dummy's are minimal. Instead, try the effect of drawing all the missing trumps (three rounds are necessary), cashing the ace of hearts and coming to hand with the ace of diamonds. At this point dummy has one trump only left but it is enough as long as it West who holds the missing king of hearts. Declarer simply leads hearts from hand, discarding from dummy, until West decides to cover with his king. Then dummy's last trump is put to good use, the South hand re-entered with the king of diamonds and the remaining hearts (now all winners) cashed. This manoeuvre is known as a ruffing finesse.

Equally it may be a suit in dummy that can be established.

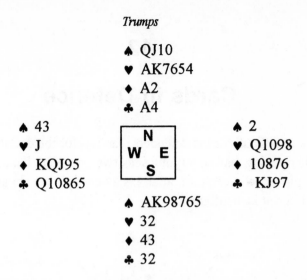

```
              ♠ QJ10
              ♥ AK7654
              ♦ A2
              ♣ A4
  ♠ 43          N         ♠ 2
  ♥ J        W     E      ♥ Q1098
  ♦ KQJ95       S         ♦ 10876
  ♣ Q10865                ♣ KJ97
              ♠ AK98765
              ♥ 32
              ♦ 43
              ♣ 32
```

Again you are South in a spade contract—how many tricks can you hope for after the lead of the king of diamonds? Seven spades, two hearts, one diamond and one club looks like only eleven and there is nothing that can be ruffed in the short trump hand. The heart suit, however, is a potential source of extra tricks. Try following this sequence of play after winning with the ace of diamonds. Draw trumps in two rounds with the queen and jack, cash the ace and king of hearts to reveal the 4-1 break and that East still has two high hearts. Ruff a heart in hand, cross to the ten of spades, and ruff another heart in hand (establishing two heart winners in dummy). Finally cross to the ace of clubs and discard your minor-suit losers on the remaining hearts. Notice that you started with seven trump tricks and made only seven trump tricks after ruffing twice in the long trump hand. But it all became worthwhile when the hearts became established and you were able to reach them. That made all thirteen tricks and leaves you wondering whether you should have bid the grand slam!

12

Cards in Defence

Life is more difficult for the defenders than it is for the declarer. Although (after the opening lead) everyone sees two complete hands, declarer is the only player who can look at all his available assets in any particular suit. So if a suit is distributed:

$$♦ AQ2$$
$$♦ 1098 \qquad\qquad ♦ 765$$
$$♦ KJ43$$

and South is declarer he knows that he has four tricks to come. If, however, North-South end up as defenders it is not immediately clear to either of them that they own between them all the high cards in the suit.

The other problem facing defenders is that they usually have fewer high cards to work with than declarer (otherwise why are they not playing the hand?). What they must try to do is to make their limited assets work for them as efficiently as possible.

If, as a defender, you are the fourth person to play to a trick you have an easy job. If the trick has already been won by your partner you do not have to worry. If so far it belongs to declarer's side and you can beat their card you do so, as cheaply as possible. If it belongs to the opponents and you can do nothing about it you have even less cause to worry!

If, as a defender, you are the third person to play to a trick, it must mean that your partner has led the suit. Normally he has led it for some good reason and you do the best you can to help him.

If you are the first person to play to a trick you have special problems which we will consider in the next chapter.

If you are the second person to play to a trick, you will not always get it right, but here are some guidelines that will put you on the right track most of the time.

Consider a very simple suit which illustrates several points:

♦ K43

♦ A76   ♦ J1098

♦ Q52

First, although we consider opening leads in far more detail later, it does not pay West to lead this suit. If he leads the ace, declarer will have no trouble in winning two tricks. Equally, if West starts by leading a low card, declarer wins the first trick with his queen and can establish a second winner in the suit by leading towards the king.

Secondly, suppose that South (the declarer) is the first to lead the suit. If he tries a low card it is not a good idea for West to rush in with his ace. This will prove just as ineffective as if he had led the ace, for all it collects is the two and the three, leaving declarer to score both his king and queen separately.

It all contributes to one of the best known adages in bridge: *second hand plays low*. It certainly works here for if West follows to the lead of the two with his six, dummy's king will win but—and this is the important point—this will be the last trick that declarer makes in the suit. A second lead from dummy brings the nine from East and leaves South with the choice of letting the nine win or playing his queen to be extinguished by the ace.

The trouble with 'second hand plays low' is that there are a number of exceptions. For example, if a suit is distributed:

♦ 103

♦ AKQJ2   ♦ 654

♦ 987

and South, the declarer, leads the seven, it would be carrying a good principle too far for West to contribute the two. A rather surprised-looking

South would find his seven winning and West would have a lot of explaining to do to his partner.

A rather more important exception arises from our earlier example:

$$\spadesuit \text{ K43}$$

$$\spadesuit \text{ A76} \qquad\qquad \spadesuit \text{ J1098}$$

$$\spadesuit \text{ Q52}$$

South starts by leading the queen. If West slavishly follows the rule and plays low, the queen wins the first trick and it is easy for declarer to come to a second trick in the suit by continuing with a low card towards the king. It leads to a refinement of our earlier advice so that it now reads: *Second hand plays low but covers an honour with an honour.* This certainly works well with our example but the phrase, *Cover an honour with an honour,* requires amplification. We are not for one moment suggesting that any useful purpose would be served by putting a queen on top of an opponent's king so, strictly speaking, 'with an honour' should read *with a higher honour.*

Take a simple example:

$$\spadesuit \text{ A32}$$

$$\spadesuit \text{ KJ10} \qquad\qquad \spadesuit \text{ 9876}$$

$$\spadesuit \text{ Q54}$$

Just suppose that South (mistakenly) started by leading the queen. Don't just say to yourself "If I cover with my king I will lose it to the ace"—think what happens after that. With the queen, king and ace out of the way you will win the next two tricks with your ten and jack.

Again:

$$\spadesuit \text{ AJ5}$$

$$\spadesuit \text{ K109} \qquad\qquad \spadesuit \text{ 432}$$

$$\spadesuit \text{ Q876}$$

Suppose that South leads the queen. First, if you play low the queen wins. South follows with a finesse of the jack, cashes the ace (on which your king falls uselessly) and ends with four tricks in the suit. Don't let declarer make tricks with his queen, jack and ace separately—cover the queen with your king! Declarer wins in dummy with the ace and can cash the jack. But who is going to win the third round of the suit? You are, with your ten. The effect of covering the queen with your king is to make declarer use two high cards, the queen and the ace, to win one trick.

Change the scene a little:

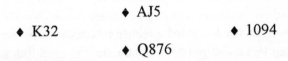

♦ AJ5

♦ K32   ♦ 1094

♦ Q876

Again South leads the queen and, just as before, if you do not cover, the queen wins the first trick, a finesse of the jack the second, and your king simply falls under the ace. But if you cover the queen with your king declarer can win the ace and take his jack but your partner will win the third round of the suit with his ten. Bridge is a partnership game and by covering with your king you promoted a trick for East and, as a result, make a friend for life.

Not unnaturally you will ask "How do I know that my partner has the ten?". You don't. But if declarer has it—perhaps:

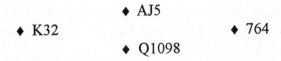

♦ AJ5

♦ K32   ♦ 764

♦ Q1098

then your side was never going to make a trick in the suit. If a play cannot lose and may gain, it is a good play.

Playing aces on kings and kings on queens is not too difficult but jacks as well can be sensible targets—for example:

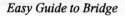

♦ AQ2

♦ K54   ♦ 10863

♦ J97

If the jack is led, covering with the king promotes a trick for East's ten on the third round of the suit.

Even the ten—which is, after all, an honour—can profitably be covered.

♦ AJ2

♦ K65   ♦ Q97

♦ 10843

Try it out—when the ten is led a failure to cover allows East to win with his queen but this is the last trick for the defenders in this suit when, later in the play, declarer finesses the jack. But if the play had started with the ten, king and ace? Then East would be left, not with just one trick for his queen, but two tricks as he has the queen and nine sitting over dummy's jack.

It is even possible to construct a suit where covering a nine (although it is not an honour) can gain:

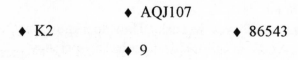

♦ AQJ107

♦ K2   ♦ 86543

♦ 9

Failure to cover the nine when it is led leads to five tricks for declarer while covering restricts him to four, East winning the fifth round with his eight!

From what we have said so far it would seem that it is always right to cover an honour with a higher honour but, alas, this is not true. There are several exceptions but they are logical and can usually be identified if you bear in mind the purpose of covering—to promote a lower-ranking card in either your hand or your partner's into trick-taking status.

Suppose that a suit (or what you can see of it from the East seat) is distributed like this:

♦ QJ109

♦ ?   ♦ K432

♦ ?

and declarer starts by leading the queen from dummy. Here covering can serve no useful purpose—if the first trick consists of the queen, king and ace it is easy to see that dummy will win the next three tricks. Indeed, covering could easily cost your side a trick:

(a)

♦ QJ109

♦ A   ♦ K432

♦ 8765

West will not be pleased with your activities when he wins your king with his ace.

(b)

♦ QJ109

♦ 65   ♦ K432

♦ A87

Nothing is to be promoted by covering and so the queen wins the first trick. The same applies when the jack is led and again it wins. East is certainly not going to be tempted by the ten for he has seen eight cards in the suit already and knows that the ace will have to be played on this trick—leaving East's king as a winner.

(c)

♦ QJ9

♦ 1054   ♦ K32

♦ A876

This one is more difficult. If East covers the queen on the first round of the suit declarer will win with his ace and follow by finessing dummy's nine successfully to make all four tricks in the suit. But if you let the queen win and cover the jack (if it follows) your partner will win the third round of the suit with his ten.

In order to get things right (most of the time) a good rule to follow is *never to cover an honour if you can see that it is supported by at least one equal card in the same hand.* So in the last example you do not cover the queen (for at the time it was led it was backed up by the jack) but on the next round you cover the jack—when the jack is led it is not reinforced by either the queen or the ten.

All very well, but the trouble is that sometimes the honour that is led is from declarer's hand and you cannot see whether it is supported or not:

♦ A3

♦ K54   ♦ ?

♦ Q?

The queen is led—do you cover or not?

You are right to do so if the suit is:

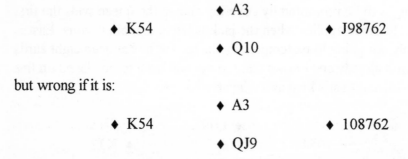

♦ A3

♦ K54   ♦ J98762

♦ Q10

but wrong if it is:

♦ A3

♦ K54   ♦ 108762

♦ QJ9

Finally, your decision whether to cover or not may be influenced by the bidding. Suppose that as East this is what you can see of the heart suit:

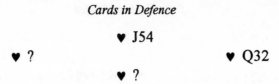

First, imagine that South has opened one heart and everyone has passed (exciting stuff!). What do you do if the jack is led from dummy? Declarer may have only a four-card suit so a cover looks best—this could be the complete suit:

♥ J54

♥ 1076 ♥ Q32

♥ AK98

and the cover promotes a trick for West's ten on the third round.

But suppose that the bidding had gone like this:

West	North	East	South
			1 ♥
Pass	1 ♠	Pass	2 ♥
Pass	3NT	Pass	4 ♥
All Pass			

Again at an early stage declarer leads the jack of trumps from dummy. You are certainly not going to promote anything in your hand by covering—is there any chance of promoting something in your partner's hand? Hardly, for South's bidding has told you that he has got at least six cards in hearts. And that leaves one card at most in West's hand. What is worse, it would be a grave mistake for you to even think about covering. Perhaps the suit is:

91

♥ J54

♥ 6   ♥ Q32

♥ AK10987

Missing only four cards in the suit declarer's normal play is simply to lead the ace and king, hoping that the missing trumps are 2-2 or that the queen will fall singleton. But it costs him nothing to lead the jack from dummy to see if you show any reaction or, better still, cover to leave him with no further problem in the suit. If you play low unblinkingly he will almost certainly play with the odds and try to drop the queen in two rounds (as he owns the ten, nine etc., the jack was of no particular value to him). Should you twitch and consult the ceiling before playing low he may well change plan and finesse successfully against your queen. (And if you think it would be a clever trick and deceptive to twitch and consult the ceiling if you had started with only the three and the two, you are right, it would be deceptive. But it would also be actively unethical and you would not be invited to play there again...)

To sum up, although with a cumbersome sentence riddled with conditional clauses:

Second hand plays low except that it should cover an unprotected honour with a higher honour except when there is no prospect of promoting a lower-ranking card in either your hand or partner's.

13

Opening Leads

Traditionally the problem of choosing an opening lead can be sticky. It is the one card that anyone plays at a time that they can only see thirteen cards. Once the lead has been made and dummy has appeared more information is available. Indeed, as the play proceeds, one likes to think that the situation becomes clearer and clearer.

Ideally a lead should have three properties. It should be *constructive*—doing something useful for the defending side. It should be *safe*—not giving the other side a trick that they could not have made if you had not led the suit. It should be *informative*—giving your partner some idea of why you led the suit and from what sort of holding. It sounds a tall order but sometimes, alas not often enough, you can satisfy all three criteria.

For example, you may have a suit headed by a sequence of touching honours:

♠ AKQ2   or
♠ KQJ7   or
♠ QJ104

First of all it is imperative and logical when you lead from such a suit to choose an honour. Otherwise the suit may lie like this:

      ♥ K53
♥ QJ104   ♥ 876
      ♥ A92

If you had led the four, declarer would have won a silly trick with his nine and would still have his ace and king in reserve. Leading an honour, however, and doing the same again when next you gain the lead, restricts declarer to his two obvious winners and your remaining honour is established as a trick.

Secondly, having decided to lead an honour, you should always *choose the top of your sequence.* Although your top cards may be equal in value, remember that you want your lead to be informative to your partner. By always leading the highest card of a sequence you put him in the picture. So if you lead the queen he knows that it is backed up with the jack and that you have not got the king in reserve.

It is worth noting that although you lead the top of a sequence, you do not play the same card if it is your partner who has led the suit. Suppose that he leads the two and this is what you can see:

The ten is the proper card to play—the lowest card that will do everything that is necessary. You may wonder why it matters—your three cards are of equal value—but suppose the complete suit is:

If you follow to the lead of the two with your queen and it loses to the ace your partner will have no idea who holds the jack and the ten, whereas if you follow to the first trick with your ten and this proves enough to force declarer's ace, your partner will know that you must hold the jack and the queen.

Already that is one good, sound lead in your repertoire—to start with the top of a sequence rarely proves wrong.

Nearly as good as a full sequence of at least three touching honours are suits headed by card combinations such as AKJ, KQ10 or QJ9. In each case there are two touching honours, followed by a gap, then the next most important card. This is nearly as constructive as a full sequence and at least partner is always sure that you have at least the next touching card. The only drawback is that it is just possible to lay out the remaining cards in such a way that your lead does not prove completely safe—perhaps:

♥ J76

♥ KQ102   ♥ 985

♥ A43

If you lead the king declarer can win with the ace and subsequently lead a low card towards dummy's jack in order to generate a second trick in the suit for his side. If you had never touched the suit in the first place, declarer could not have come to more than one trick. You had to be pretty unlucky, though, to find the rest of the suit so unkindly placed for you—the jack and at least two low cards on your left and the ace on your right. In all other circumstances your lead would have proved safe.

The trouble is that you often find yourself on lead with no trace of a sequence heading any of your suits and, as the laws of the game insist that you have to lead something, there is the question of which card you should choose from a suit of perhaps:

♥ Q10853

The standard practice is to lead the fourth highest—in this case the five. There are technical arguments both for and against this principle, but as it is followed successfully by the vast majority of players it is an excellent idea for you and your partner to stick to it. Consider some of the obvious advantages—suppose, for example, that you are defending against a no-trump contract (where it is normal to lead from a long suit) and your partner leads a two. Relying on this being his fourth highest—in other words, he has precisely three higher cards—you can place him with exactly four cards in the suit. And, as you can see how many cards both you and dummy have in the suit, it is easy to work out how many cards declarer holds. As a result you can start to form a picture of declarer's distribution—so vital when you are in defence.

It does not have to be the two from partner before you can see what is happening—he might lead the five, say, and (between you and dummy) you can see all three of the 'missing' lower cards. As a result you can place your partner with only a four-card suit.

Sometimes you have to wait a trick or two before you can be sure of what is happening in a suit. Partner leads the three of a suit and you cannot see the two—he may have only four cards in the suit, he may have five. Until the two makes its appearance you cannot be sure—if it turns up in partner's hand, he had started with a five-card suit; if it turns up elsewhere, he started with only four cards.

So far all the advice above relates equally to no-trump contracts and suit contracts but there is a very real difference in your motives. *Against a no-trump contract your aim is to establish your long suit and to get your low cards working for your side.* For example, you lead the five from ♥ Q10853 and find the suit:

Your partner's king loses to declarer's ace and, if it your partner who next gains the lead, the return of his two gives you no fewer than four tricks in the suit. Had something been trumps, however, although the play in the suit may start in the same way, you will only score two tricks with your ten and queen. Any further leads of the suit will simply be trumped by declarer or dummy and, just a tiny change, if the suit had been:

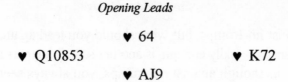

♥ 64

♥ Q10853   ♥ K72

♥ AJ9

although you still have four potential tricks against no-trumps, you now have only one if there happens to be a trump suit—dummy is able to ruff the third round of the suit.

Can you see the vital difference? Against a no-trump contract you have hopes of bringing in the whole suit; against a suit contract your ambition is limited to what you can achieve with one or two of your top cards. There is no difference in your choice of lead with a suit of Q10853, but your aims are very different. Bearing this in mind, which card would you lead from a suit of AK853? Against no-trumps, routine, you choose the fourth highest. Perhaps the suit is distributed:

♥ 1076

♥ AK853   ♥ 42

♥ QJ9

After the lead of the five, won by declarer, it does not matter whether East or West next gains the lead—the defenders have four tricks ready to cash. It is worth noting that if West had started with the ace, king and another of his suit, the defenders would certainly have two more tricks ready to take—but only if West, rather than either defender, next gained the lead.

Now suppose that one of the other suits is trumps. The lead of a low card achieves absolutely nothing, indeed West would be extremely lucky still to come to two tricks in the suit—but as he only expects to make two tricks in the suit, why not simply start with the ace and king? There is indeed a bonus if the cards lie as above—after the ace and king have been cashed, a third round of the suit allows East to ruff, yielding a third trick for the defenders and getting them off to an excellent start.

Next, suppose that your suit is A10853. As usual, the five is the right choice against no-trumps, but what should you lead against a suit contract? The answer, oddly enough, is another suit altogether! If you choose a low card, as though against no-trumps, you always seem to find the suit distributed:

♥ 764

♥ A10853   ♥ QJ92

♥ K

and, after a surprised declarer has been allowed to win the first trick with his singleton king, you find your ace being trumped later in the play. And if, to avoid this trap, you choose to lead the ace the picture may prove to be:

♥ 76

♥ A10853   ♥ QJ92

♥ K4

As a result, although your ace is not trumped, declarer later makes a completely undeserved trick with his king. It is a suit where, if only you had waited until your partner, or declarer himself, had led it, the defenders would make two tricks instead of just one. In fact, you should go so far as to make it a Golden Rule:

NEVER UNDERLEAD ACES AGAINST A SUIT CONTRACT.

If you make a habit of doing so undoubtedly you will meet with an occasional success but you will have countless disasters!

There are a number of suit combinations from which it is inadvisable to lead. If you held AQ10, where would you prefer to be sitting at the table when a trick is played in the suit? In the fourth position (or 'last in hand'), of course, and if you could arrange for this to happen twice you would be guaranteed three tricks in the suit. If you had to lead it yourself, however, your queen might lose to the king and your ten to the jack, leaving you with only one trick.

Note that this advice does not apply nearly so strictly against no-trumps if you have length in the suit as well. Leading the five from AQ1053 may cost a trick unnecessarily but the trick sacrificed may come back with interest when you are able to run your long suit. This will not happen against a suit contract—you might easily give away a trick and it will be a trick that is unlikely to come back.

So far we have discussed good leads against no-trump contracts—long suits either broken or headed by a sequence—and good leads against suit contracts—broken suits (as long as they are not headed by the ace) and sequences. There is, however, another class of leads that can be effective when defending against suit contracts. There are short-suit leads—either a singleton or a doubleton—and they would clearly not be of much help to the defence against no-trumps!

The lead of a singleton can certainly be described as constructive—if your partner has the ace of the suit led or is able to return it before all of your trumps have been drawn, the defenders will have come to an extra trick. It is not always an automatic choice—you have to think about the trump that you hope to use for ruffing. So with:

♠ 9842
♥ A32
♦ 7
♣ J9753

(where the lead of the five of clubs would be natural after the bidding of 1NT—3NT) the seven of diamonds looks a promising attack if the bidding had gone 1♥—4♥. Your two and three of trumps are not going to make tricks unless you can ruff something with them. Contrast this with:

♠ 9842
♥ KQ10
♦ 7
♣ J9753

and now (after 1♥—4♥) there would be little point in leading the singleton diamond. It seems extremely likely that you have two natural trump tricks and there is no need for you to strive for what appears to be a completely unnecessary ruff or two.

Leading a doubleton has the same motivation behind it but is a more optimistic effort than selecting a singleton. You need to find a little more in partner's hand before you can successfully take an immediate ruff; perhaps both the ace and king, or the ace and queen sitting over dummy's king. When leading a doubleton, always choose the higher of your two cards.

There is the worrying point that if after leading a short suit you fail to secure a ruff, your efforts may succeed in damaging whatever your partner held in the suit. For example, with:

♥ K962

♥ 83   ♥ Q754

♥ AJ10

leading the eight does not lead to a defensive ruff and only has the effect of picking up your partner's queen for declarer. If he had been left to play the suit himself he might easily have lost a trick.

Remember our three requirements for the perfect opening lead? *Safe, Constructive and Informative*. The lead of a doubleton can easily prove unsafe but (look on the bright side, two out of three is not too bad!) it has the other properties.

Sometimes you find yourself faced with a lead problem where opening up any of the four suits looks unattractive. For example, with:

♠ 863
♥ Q64
♦ KJ7
♣ AJ84

you find yourself on lead after the bidding:

North	South
1♣	1♥
2♥	All Pass

Take it suit by suit. A club lead, from a suit headed by the ace and bid on your left, is almost sure to work badly. A diamond lead does not appeal—it is the sort of suit that a defender far prefers someone else to open up. Often there is no objection to leading trumps but here it could so easily give up a trick in the suit—declarer will know that the queen is missing but he will not know whether it is you or your partner who holds it. Furthermore, even if he guesses you hold it, he may not be able to do anything about it (unless you have been kind enough to lead the suit!)

That leaves only the spades and you have neither the singleton nor the doubleton that would make leading the suit purposeful. Nevertheless, leading a spade is less damaging than the alternatives, and the question hinges on which card. In some parts of the world, oddly enough, the lowest card is fashionable but here the choice lies between the highest (Top of Nothing) and the middle card (MUD—Middle-Up-Down). The logic behind the latter scheme is that the second card produced by the leader (on a subsequent trick) clarifies to his partner what the lead was all about. So if the six were led and followed by the three, the lead would be identifiable as a doubleton, whereas if the six were followed by the eight the leader's partner would appreciate that the lead was from three low cards and would not, for example, attempt to secure a ruff for his side on the third round of the suit.

It sounds beautiful and logical in theory but has one slight drawback in practice—the leader's partner may not always be able to identify immediately what the lead is all about. There is a big difference between the fourth-highest card in a suit and the highest card in the suit, but less of a clear-cut distinction between a fourth-highest lead and a MUD lead. This is why a great many players adhere to the traditional Top of Nothing approach.

Suppose that you are East in the following examples. In each case your partner leads the five and, after dummy appears, you have to decide what his lead is all about.

(i)   ♠ AQ2

        ♠ 5   ♠ K43

As you can see all of the lower cards, this must be partner's fourth highest. The only other explanation—that the lead is a singleton—can almost certainly be ruled out by the bidding. If declarer had a six-card suit, you would have heard something about it!

(ii)   ♠ AQ86

        ♠ 5   ♠ K109

As there are only two cards higher than the five that you cannot see (the jack and the seven) you can rule out the possibility of the lead being fourth highest. So the lead is top of nothing (Two cards? Three cards?) but unlikely to be a singleton as this would mean that declarer held five cards in the suit.

(iii)   ♠ AQ8

        ♠ 5   ♠ K76

Apparently more difficult—it could be the top of nothing easily enough but there are three cards higher than the five that are out of sight. It is only when you think what these are—the jack, the ten and the nine—that you realise that partner's lead cannot be fourth highest. For from ♠J1095 he would have led the jack—the top of a sequence. And so his lead must be top of nothing.

There is one major factor that should always influence your choice of lead—has your partner made a bid? So often, especially if his bid was an overcall rather than an opening bid, it may have been directed towards telling you what he would like you to lead. As he may well have taken some risk in the bidding to tell you this, it seems only polite to oblige!

Having had the choice of suit made for you, it means that sometimes you will be leading from holdings in suits that otherwise you would not have tackled. Often everything is as normal—top of a sequence, fourth highest from a broken holding, top of nothing—but with two touching honours in a three-card suit (KQx, QJx, J10x) you should lead the higher of the two honours. These are suits you might easily not have led if you had been left to your own devices. With any doubleton honour (Ax, Kx, Qx, Jx, 10x) you should lead the honour. These would have been highly speculative leads had your partner not bid the suit. Singletons of course, come in all shapes and sizes and even singleton honours become attractive.

One more stranger joins the list of possibles—three-card suit headed by an honour. It is an old wives' take that you should lead your highest card in your partner's suit—this only applies when you have a sequence, nothing, a doubleton or a singleton. *The general principle is that the lead of a low card suggests an original holding of three or more cards including something of interest; the lead of a highish-looking card denies anything more important.* So with K72, Q72, J72 or even 1072 you should lead the two (remember, the ten is an honour). It is easy to see how this can help—for example:

Suppose South is declarer in no-trumps and West leads the queen, his partner having bid the suit? No matter what East does, South now has two potential tricks in the suit. But if West had led the two to his partner's ace and the suit had been returned, declarer would end with only one trick in the suit.

Whole books and countless articles have been devoted to selecting opening leads. However long you play, you will never achieve a 100% success rate! All I can suggest is that if you follow the advice above you will avoid some of the commoner pitfalls. It is an area where a great deal can be learnt only by experience.

14

Two Clubs

So far every bid that we have discussed has been completely natural—we have only bid suits that we wanted to suggest as trumps, we have only bid no-trumps if we were happy to play in no-trumps.

In some situations, however, it pays to use a bid in a conventional sense—in other words you do not necessarily have length in the suit that you name. Not just any bid, of course, for the result would be chaos—just a few. It is extremely important not to use a *convention* unless you and your partner have agreed to do so before play starts. Equally important is to make sure that your opponents know that you have this arrangement. Everything in the bidding has to be completely above board—a few conventional bids are permitted but only if they are fully explained to the other side. Two popular conventions that we shall meet later are *Stayman* (a response of two clubs to your partner's opening bid of 1NT) and *Blackwood* (a bid of 4NT in the middle of the auction). Our first introduction to a convention arises from the problems posed by an extremely strong hand. Suppose that you deal yourself:

> ♠ AKQ4
> ♥ AKQ3
> ♦ AKJ8
> ♣ 4

where practically any collection of garbage in your partner's hand will still enable you to make a game. The trouble is that if you open one spade, one heart or one diamond, on many hands partner will simply pass and there you will languish. Now, your hand is certainly strong enough to insist on game but which game? Here are three terrible hands that your partner may hold:

(a) ♠ J862   (b) ♠ 65   (c) ♠ 65
    ♥ 65   ♥ J862   ♥ 65
    ♦ 652   ♦ 653   ♦ 109753
    ♣ 8762   ♣ 8762   ♣ 8762

Facing (a) you have an easy four spades, with (b) an equally easy four
hearts while with (c) you would be delighted to end in five diamonds. How,
then, can you find out which hand partner holds? Blind guesswork will
work only a fraction of the time!

The solution is to open *two clubs—a conventional bid that bears
no relation whatsoever to your holding in clubs but carries the message "Partner, on my own I expect to make game"*. UNDER NO
CIRCUMSTANCES *stop bidding until we have reached a game.* Note
that it is only the *opening bid* of two clubs that carries any special
significance—if partner opens (say) one spade and you respond two clubs,
this is a perfectly normal bid. If the opponent on your right opens one
heart and you join in with two clubs, this is a perfectly normal bid.

The responder to two clubs has a conventional reply which he will make
with all of the above three hands. It is a negative *two diamonds,* a response showing a poor hand and bearing no relation to his length or strength
in diamonds.

He does not have to make the negative bid two diamonds—with fair
values (seven/eight points or more) he gives a 'positive' response rather
than a 'negative'. This takes the form of bidding any respectable suit or,
with a reasonably balanced hand with no great suit, 2NT. Examples of
positive responses would be:

(a) ♠ AQJ74   (b) ♠ 832   (c) ♠ Q107
    ♥ 653   ♥ 974   ♥ 8542
    ♦ 82   ♦ 85   ♦ A94
    ♣ 1074   ♣ AKJ63   ♣ Q9

With (a) bid two spades, with (b) three clubs, and with (c) 2NT. What about:

$$(d) \quad \spadesuit \; 832$$
$$\heartsuit \; 974$$
$$\diamondsuit \; AKJ63$$
$$\clubsuit \; 85$$

Take care: not two diamonds, which is the conventional negative, but *three* diamonds. After these starts the rest of the bidding is completely natural with one exception. Consider these two hands:

West	**East**
♠ AK974	♠ 82
♥ AKJ3	♥ 10974
♦ 4	♦ J85
♣ AKQ	♣ 9632

There is no difficulty with the start—West opens two clubs, East bids two diamonds, and West rebids two spades. Now East has a problem—he cannot support spades, he has no suit of his own worth mentioning, and yet he cannot pass! The solution is to *follow his negative of two diamonds with 2NT—a 'second negative'*. It completes the picture of his abysmal hand—little or nothing in high cards, no support for his partner's suit, and no worthwhile suit of his own. There is still no hurry (the partnership are both committed to reaching game) so West shows his second suit with three hearts and East raises to four hearts (with a sigh of relief that he will not be expected to make any more bids on his collection of tram tickets).

Again, East's hand might have been:

$$\spadesuit \; 842$$
$$\heartsuit \; 74$$
$$\diamondsuit \; 9763$$
$$\clubsuit \; 9632$$

107

and again the auction starts:

West	East
2♣	2♦
2♠	2NT
3♥	?

Now East's next bid is three spades, and he has shown a poor hand with no direct support for either of his partner's suits (and no suit of his own) but—and this is the key factor—he *prefers* his partner's spades to his hearts. Quite simply 'prefers' means 'holds more cards in' with no relation to whether high cards are held or not. With this assurance West can go on to game in spades, confident that he has found a sensible trump suit.

To complete our summary of responding to two clubs, how should East bid his hand if he is responding with:

♠ 4
♥ 85
♦ QJ9762
♣ J1093

First two diamonds (negative) but then, if partner bids two spades, three diamonds—showing the suit for the first time. Now if partner continues with three hearts, 3NT ("I have a guard in clubs as well as the reasonable diamond suit that I have shown; I do not like either of your suits") completes the description of his hand.

Finally, perhaps a little illogically, let us come back to the decision of what constitutes a two-club opening. 'Enough for game on your own' is a little vague. Perhaps the best way to define it is to imagine that partner has balanced rubbish, that all your long suits are breaking reasonably well round the table and, as a result, it looks as though you will make enough tricks for game. Note well that the precise number of points that you hold does not come into it, but that you should have a good ration of aces and kings—*defensive* values as well as *offensive* values. So with:

♠ KQJ10973
♥ QJ10942
♦ None
♣ None

you certainly expect to make game on your own but you are very poor in high cards and have little or no defence if the opponents outbid you. As a result, you reject the possibility of opening two clubs. Equally, with:

♠ AK74
♥ A83
♦ A74
♣ A62

you are bristling with aces and kings but cannot possibly develop enough tricks for game unless you get a certain amount of co-operation from partner.
However:

♠ AKQJ1074
♥ AK63
♦ None
♣ K5

certainly qualifies. You may wonder why, with such a magnificent spade suit, you do not just open four spades and save time. The answer is that you would like to find out if partner holds anything useful when a small slam or even a grand slam (with their attendant bonuses!) may be available. Obviously if partner displays no interest at all you will end up in four spades.

There remains one problem—the hand which has a very high point-count but is balanced, so that counting likely winners is much more difficult. For example:

♠ AK74
♥ AQ6
♦ AQ3
♣ AJ9

24 points but only five certain winners. The solution is that you still open *two clubs* but, after the likely response of two diamonds, you rebid *2NT*. *This is the ONLY sequence in which, in spite of the two-club opening, the partnership can stop short of game.* Two clubs followed by 2NT shows a balanced 23-24 points and partner can pass—just!—if he has practically nothing. An odd queen and a jack is more than enough for him to go on to game.

You could be lucky enough to be dealt an even stronger balanced hand, say:

♠ AK76
♥ AK6
♦ AK3
♣ AJ9

still only seven certain tricks, but now 26 points. You open two clubs and, after the almost inevitable negative reply, rebid 3NT. This describes a balanced hand with 25-26 points.

With an even stronger balanced hand (you should be so lucky!) you have to improvise by opening two clubs and following with a suit call. This, as you remember, commits your side to bidding game and at least you will hear if partner has anything at all of interest before you plunge to 3NT.

15

Other Opening Bids of Two

Between the hands that are ordinary opening bids of one of a suit and the dramatic, forcing to game two-club openers, there are hands which are very close to game but need some support from partner. The danger is that if they are opened with one of a suit partner may not have enough to respond (6 or more points) and yet has the necessary bits and pieces to make game a good proposition. Equally if, feeling optimistic, you decide to open two clubs you may find him with absolutely nothing. Duty bound by your opening, however, he will be constrained to continue bidding until a hopeless game has been reached.

A typical problem hand would be:

> ♠ KQ4
> ♥ AKQ763
> ♦ AQ2
> ♣ 5

If you found your partner with:

(a)		(b)	
♠	753	♠	A763
♥	852	♥	852
♦	974	♦	97
♣	10863	♣	10863

you would make eight tricks with hearts as trumps (nine if lucky) with (a) as dummy, but eleven (or even twelve!) with (b).

The halfway house between opening two clubs and one heart is to open two hearts. This suggests a good six-card (or longer) heart suit and the expectation, facing rubbish, of generating eight or nine tricks.

While an opening bid of two clubs is (in principle) forcing to game, *an opening bid of two of any other suit is natural and forcing for one round only.* With the sort of hand that would have passed an opening bid of one heart—hands (a) and (b) above are good examples—responder bids *2NT—a negative reply,* very similar to the two-diamond response to two clubs. The difference is that if the opener merely rebids his own suit, the responder is free to pass. That is just what he does with (a) over a rebid of three hearts but (b) is altogether a different matter. In support of hearts he has no fewer than three possibly useful features—an ace, three trumps, and a doubleton elsewhere. They may not all be working but together they make the hand worth a comfortable raise of three hearts to four.

You may wonder why, if the opening bid suggests only eight or nine playing tricks, responder should be forced to keep the bidding open with a very poor hand. It is because the opener may have another suit that he wishes to show—and this may suit responder much better. Take this pair of hands:

West	East
♠ AKQ743	♠ 2
♥ A	♥ 10873
♦ AQ64	♦ K10973
♣ 42	♣ 1085

West opens two spades and, with very little interest, East replies 2NT. But when West follows with three diamonds, East brightens up and the partnership should now end in five diamonds.

As with opening bids of two clubs, the precise number of points that you hold does not come into the decision whether to open one or two of your suit.

♠ AKJ
♥ J8763
♦ AKQ5
♣ K

has 21 high-card points but the suit is not good enough for two hearts—you have to settle for one heart and hope that you will get another chance. By contrast:

♠ AK64
♥ AKQ1095
♦ 63
♣ 2

has only 16 high-card points but it is an excellent two-heart opening bid!

If you are thinking clearly, one problem will occur to you— what do you open with:

♠ 4
♥ QJ10
♦ AK7
♣ AKQJ97

It looks like nine playing tricks with clubs as trumps, but you cannot open two clubs for this, as you remember, conventionally insists on game. This is the penalty that you pay for making any particular bid conventional—you can no longer use it as a natural bid!

With the hand above, your best bet is to open one club and hope that the next three players do not pass! Even if they do, it is quite possible that you have not missed anything.

There is one more strong opening bid to add to our armoury—an opening of *2NT*. Like all no-trump bids this shows a balanced hand and so the point count becomes significant. A typical hand for the bid would be:

♠ AQ6
♥ AK74
♦ A83
♣ A105

and the range is *20-22 points*. Although the bid is clearly a strong one it is not forcing, and partner with nothing is quite free to pass. Nevertheless, he does not need much to go on to game.

In reply to an opening bid of 1NT, you will remember, if you did not like no-trumps you could bid two of a long suit (warning partner to pass) or three of a long suit (insisting on game). In reply to 2NT, however, there is less room to manoeuvre. Although you may come across different ideas later, the simplest approach is to treat *any* responses to 2NT as forcing to game—you will only bid a suit if you hold at least five cards in it. The only way of putting on the brakes short of game is to pass 2NT.

16

Three and Higher Bids

We have considered all of the possible opening bids at the one and two level, but there remains the possibility of starting operations at a higher level. Your instinctive feeling will be that, if opening at the one level is normal and opening at the two level is strong, then an opening of three should be very strong indeed. This, however, is not the case for we have seen that extremely powerful hands are always introduced with an opening bid of two clubs—effectively establishing a game-forcing situation and leaving plenty of room to find out what, if anything, partner holds.

The whole object of a three bid is completely different—it is designed, purely and simply, to annoy your opponents. It is called a *pre-emptive bid*. Suppose, for example, you are the dealer with:

♠ KQJ10743
♥ 64
♦ 842
♣ 5

Even allowing for your seven-card suit, you have nothing like the values necessary for an opening bid of one spade. If you pass, you have given your opponents a clear run and—more often than not—they will reach their right contract. Furthermore, your hand contains very little defence against anything they can reach—if you are lucky you may come to a spade trick. It is an ideal hand with which to try to put a spanner in their works and you should open three spades. Now they will have to start their bidding at the four level and—with so little bidding space in which to explore—may easily end in the wrong contract.

Of course, on your own you do not expect to make three spades for you can only guarantee six tricks in spades and nothing else. It has all the hallmarks of a disaster if your partner turns up with, say:

♠ 962
♥ J52
♦ 975
♣ 10862

for you will certainly not be allowed to play in three spades undoubled and will lose the obvious seven tricks to go three down. Oddly enough, you would be delighted if this happened for it is practically impossible to construct hands for your opponents with which they will not have a an easy grand slam in hearts, diamonds, clubs or even no-trumps! Which would you rather do—lose 500 points in three spades doubled, or lose three or four times as many points watching them bid and make their grand slam?

There are three aspects of pre-emptive bidding to consider:

I   Choosing the right hand and the right level at which to pre-empt
II   Responding if your partner pre-empts
III   Taking action against an opposing pre-empt.

I Choosing the right hand and the right level at which to pre-empt
Nobody will always choose the right time—it may be that it is your partner who has a strong hand and it is your side's bidding space that is being used up. At least you don't have to worry about this if your partner has already passed. Flair or intuition undoubtedly comes into it but some useful guidelines are as follows:

(a) Your hand should not be strong enough to open with one of your suit.

(b) You should always hold seven or more cards in your suit—ensuring tricks if your suit is trumps but of little value in defence.

(c) Of your strictly limited values, most should be in your long suit. This means that your suit should be good. With ♥ KQJ10974 you can guarantee six tricks if hearts are trumps but if your suit is only as good as, say, ♥K1086432 you might end with perhaps only two tricks from your suit if the adverse cards are unkindly placed. So with:

♠ QJ10
♥ K1086432
♦ Q5
♣ 4

you would be better advised to pass rather than open three hearts. Some authorities suggest that your pre-emptive bid should show 6-10 points, but this is perhaps too rigid. If you stick to the idea of a good seven-card suit with little of value outside you will not go far wrong.

(d) If your partner has not already passed, do not pre-empt if you have four cards in a major suit as well as your seven-card suit. Just suppose that you had opened three diamonds with the West hand below and that your side held:

West	East
♠ 10864	♠ AK97
♥ 4	♥ A763
♦ AQ109763	♦ 5
♣ 5	♣ AK82

The effect of pre-empting would be that your side ends in a bad five diamonds or a worse 3NT instead of the good contract of four spades.

When your partner has already passed—and thus cannot possibly hold a good hand, so that you can be reasonably sure that your opponents have a good chance of making game—you can take more liberties, and with the West hand above there would be no objections to pre-empting.

(e) Another factor which comes into the decision-making is the vulner-ability. If your side has made a game, the penalties for going off (doubled or not) are more severe. An old suggestion—some fifty years old!—is called the 'Rule of 2 and 3' or the 'Rule of 500'. It suggests that if you are not vulnerable you are prepared to go three off doubled (losing 500 points) but that if you are vulnerable you should be within two tricks of your target (again losing 500 points if you are doubled).

Consider these two hands:

	(i)		(ii)
♠	KQJ10743	♠	KQJ10743
♥	65	♥	65
♦	842	♦	QJ10
♣	5	♣	5

Hand (i) is fine for opening three spades if you are not vulnerable but the extra trick that you are likely to develop in diamonds makes hand (ii) more suitable for vulnerable pre-emption.

It is a sound enough idea but the modern tendency—to put as much pressure on the opponents as often as possible—leads to most players adopting a rather more freewheeling approach, especially when non-vul-nerable.

The rule is more effective when deciding between opening with three or four of a suit for, as you may have guessed, an opening of four (or even five) is still a pre-emptive bid. For example

♠ KQJ108652
♥ 7
♦ 4
♣ QJ9

would be a sensible opening bid of four spades at any vulnerability, while with:

♠ 5
♥ 4
♦ AKJ965432
♣ K5

five diamonds suggests itself.

What about opening bids of 3NT and 4NT? 3NT does not show a balanced 25-26 points for, as you will remember, hands like these are described by opening two clubs and rebidding 3NT. Rather ingeniously, it shows a completely solid seven-card minor suit with very little outside. Partner is expected to pass with guards in three suits—with which he will know what your suit is, for he cannot have a guard in a suit where you have all the honours! or to bid four clubs if he has two or more unguarded suits. This you either pass or, if diamonds are your suit, convert to four diamonds. In effect you have opened with a minor-suit pre-empt at the four level, forcing the opponents to take action at a high level if they wish to compete, without going past the possible game contract of 3NT for your side.

A typical hand would be:

♠ Q3
♥ 84
♦ 76
♣ AKQJ1062

Your partner will pass 3NT with, say:

♠ A652
♥ QJ5
♦ A843
♣ 83

119

but will convert to four clubs with:

♠ KJ94
♥ A765
♦ 852
♣ 83

An opening bid of 4NT is very much of a rarity—it is not Blackwood, for no suit has been agreed, but it does ask about your partner's aces (if any). He is expected to tell you which aces he holds rather than how many. His replies are:

Five clubs	no aces
Five diamonds	the ace of diamonds
Five hearts	the ace of hearts
Five spades	the ace of spades
5NT	two aces
Six clubs	the ace of clubs

So with (you should be so lucky!)

♠ AKQJ1064
♥ AKQ
♦ None
♣ KQ

you open 4NT. Over replies of five clubs or five diamonds you know that the ace of clubs is missing and you settle for six spades. If, however, partner responds six clubs you can bid seven spades with confidence and over 5NT you can bid 7NT and give ourselves the pleasure of claiming thirteen tricks before the opening lead has been made!

A final thought about pre-emptive openings—only to be played after previous discussion with your partner!—is a convention called, rather bafflingly, *South African Texas.* It means giving up four-level pre-empts in the minor suits, because four clubs and four diamonds show *good* pre-emptive bids in hearts and spades respectively. So with:

♠ KQJ108642
♥ 7
♦ 4
♣ QJ9

you still open four spades, but with:

♠ AKQJ9863
♥ K4
♦ 72
♣ 5

you open four diamonds. You have quite enough to open one spade (or even two spades) but you have extremely little in defence and—as usual—would prefer your opponents to do their guesswork at as high a level as possible.

Whatever you do, do not bring this weapon into play unless you are quite sure your partner understands!

II Responding if your partner pre-empts

Usually the answer is quite simple—you pass! You must bear in mind that partner is several tricks short of making his contract—to make any advance you must hold quite significant values.

Always picture your partner with something like:

♠ 74
♥ KQJ10853
♦ 62
♣ 95

and ask yourself where you are going with:

♠ AK32
♥ 2
♦ A754
♣ A842

You can supply four tricks—three will be used up for partner to make his contract but your extra one justifies a shot at game. What game? Whatever you do, you must resist the temptation to bid 3NT. It is no good saying "He has the hearts, I have the other three suits guarded"—you must ask "Where are the tricks coming from?". Not hearts, certainly, for you will never be able to use partner's long suit in no-trumps, and you obviously cannot produce nine winners on your own. The right answer, of course, is to raise to four hearts—then the long hearts will be working. Note too that you need quick tricks—aces and kings—to go on. It is not just the fact that you have 15 points that excites you—with:

♠ QJ105
♥ 2
♦ KQJ4
♣ KQJ2

you still have 15 points but you will not even make three hearts, let alone four.

This does not mean that you should never bid 3NT in response to a pre-empt. There are two types of hand on which it is sound to do so. Suppose you hear partner open three diamonds. Perhaps he holds:

♠ J3
♥ 953
♦ KQ109872
♣ 5

With:

♠ Q109
♥ KJ4
♦ AJ3
♣ AK62

You can certainly bid 3NT—you have the unbid suits well guarded and—the key factor—you know that you will be able to run seven diamond tricks when you get in because of your excellent fit in partner's suit.

Alternatively, you might bid 3NT with:

♠ K52
♥ K10
♦ None
♣ AKQJ9862

Now, with the opening lead coming round to you, you expect to make nine tricks on your own.

It all leads to a golden rule: *If you have pre-empted and your partner bids 3NT—Pass.* He knows what he is doing and may have either of the hand types above. A retreat to four of your own suit, be it major or minor, betrays a complete lack of trust in your partner's judgement.

Every so often your partner chooses quite the wrong moment to pre-empt, catching you with a strong distributional hand. A jump to game in your own suit is sometimes available—over three diamonds you would bid four spades with:

♠ KQJ10763
♥ A4
♦ 63
♣ AQ

and expect to have a fair chance of success. Life would be more difficult with:

♠ AK1042
♥ AQJ84
♦ None
♣ KJ4

and the best bet would be to start with three spades, planning to show your hearts on the next round if your spades are not supported. Partner will make every effort to support you—a bid of a new suit by you over partner's pre-empt is forcing. One thing is certain—you have a good hand. Never bother to set up in competition with partner's known good seven-card suit when you have only moderate values. So with:

♠ A97432
♥ KJ6
♦ None
♣ KJ43

leave his bid of three diamonds well alone—remember he cannot pass three spades if you bid it.

III Taking action against an opposing pre-empt

Straightaway it must be admitted that joining in at the three level is always attended with some risk and there is no perfect answer to all of your problems. After all, that is why your opponent has pre-empted—to make life difficult for you! A variety of alternatives have been suggested, tried and usually rejected, but by far the most popular is the one which is also the simplest and probably the best.

(a) With a fair six-card suit and reasonable values simply overcall. Partner will appreciate that you were under pressure and will not rely on you having nine certain tricks. So with:

♠ KJ10875	or	♠ A82
♥ AJ		♥ KQJ973
♦ 42		♦ K5
♣ AK4		♣ Q9

try three spades and three hearts respectively.

(b) With a strong balanced hand or a long suit that is likely to run, and with a fair guard in the opponent's suit, try 3NT. Either of these two hands would be suitable for a bid of 3NT if your right-hand opponent opens three diamonds:

♠ AQ4	or	♠ J5
♥ KJ9		♥ A62
♦ AJ6		♦ K4
♣ KJ103		♣ AKQ1097

Your partner will not usually disturb this call unless he is either strong (when he might go on to a slam) or very distributional. Remember that you have not invited him to bid, which brings us to the third possibility...

(c) With a fair hand with shortage in the opponent's suit and values in the other three suits, make a take-out double. In essence this is just the same as a take-out double of one of a suit and it strongly suggests that your partner should bid something. Over three diamonds a double would be best with

♠ AK64
♥ AQ83
♦ 2
♣ KJ102

Normally partner will reply in his longest suit, jumping to game if he has reasonable values. He may also try 3NT or even pass your double for penalties if he has tricks in the trump suit but not much elsewhere. So with:

(a) ♠ QJ1093   (b) ♠ QJ10973   (c) ♠ 932   (d) ♠ 932
    ♥ 752   ♥ K7   ♥ 764   ♥ 76
    ♦ 1053   ♦ 1053   ♦ QJ109   ♦ KQ10
    ♣ 95   ♣ Q9   ♣ A743   ♣ AQ976

his responses would be three spades, four spades, no bid and 3NT respectively.

You have been warned that no method is perfect. Over three diamonds you might find yourself looking at:

                    ♠ 3
                    ♥ A542
                    ♦ AQJ9
                    ♣ QJ102

You are quite sure that they will not make three diamonds, but a double by you would risk your partner jumping to game in spades. Nor would you be on firm ground in trying 3NT. All that you can do is pass and, if your partner can take no action, be satisfied with a small plus score.

17

Slam Bidding

There is a great deal of satisfaction in bidding (and making!) a slam. Apart from the aesthetic pleasure there are also the extra points scored.

Small slams (successful contracts of six) earn bonuses of 500 points when non-vulnerable and 750 points when vulnerable.

Grand slams (successful contracts of seven) collect corresponding bonuses of 1,000 and 1,500 points.

There are three ways in which a slam can be reached—via Bashing, Blackwood or Cue-bidding; hence the mnemonic BBC. Each way has its advantages and disadvantages and the ideal solution is to have all three methods in your armoury but only to use them on the right hands. It is choosing the right hands that poses the problems!

Bashing

Bashing appeals to the gambler—it may or may not lead to the academically correct contract but even if you end in what appears to be an impossible slam you may still succeed if an opponent finds the wrong lead. And, by bashing, you have given him no clues at all.

Suppose that you open one spade with:

♠ AQ6542
♥ 432
♦ AKQ10
♣ None

your partner raises to three spades and you 'bash' six spades. If your partner holds:

♠ K1087
♥ A86
♦ J74
♣ K65

you find that (luckily) you have landed in the right contract and will succeed no matter what is led. If however he holds:

♠ K1087
♥ AK6
♦ J74
♣ 652

you will find yourself making all thirteen tricks no matter what is led and you are left wondering whether a more scientific approach might have led you to the grand slam. Finally, partner may turn up with:

♠ K1087
♥ 865
♦ J74
♣ AK6

You will make only ten tricks if the opponents lead hearts and continue the suit, but on any other lead you will make your small slam. But, after a more delicate approach, you would almost certainly have directed the opening leader's attention to your weakness in hearts.

Blackwood
This is one of the oldest of bidding conventions. As it is so simple it is very popular and, as a result, used far too much, often on quite unsuit-

able hands. It was first described by the late Easley Blackwood over fifty years ago, and (in the fashion in which new, good ideas are often treated) it was scorned by the bridge authorities of the time. Only later did its virtues, when used on the right hands, become universally acknowledged.

The principle involved is simple. When a suit has been agreed and a player has good reason to suspect that the partnership holds the combined values to make twelve or more tricks possible, a bid of 4NT asks partner how many aces he holds—not which aces, but *how many* aces. There are a number of variants but in the original (and most widely played) version, partner replies as follows:

> Five clubs shows no aces
> Five diamonds shows one ace
> Five hearts shows two aces
> Five spades shows three aces

If, and only if, the reply is satisfactory the Blackwood bidder can continue with 5NT, asking about the number of kings held by partner, who bases his replies on the same schedule as before but one level higher. So:

> Six clubs shows no kings
> Six diamonds shows one king
> Six hearts shows two kings
> Six spades shows three kings

Note well the phrase '*if, and only if,* the reply is satisfactory'. The continuation of 5NT absolutely guarantees that the partnership between them hold all four aces. This is very logical for if an ace is missing you do not want to be in a grand slam as, whatever the reply to 5NT, the partnership will end by playing at the six level.

You may wonder whether it is possible to hold all four aces and yet hear your partner ask about aces and, if so, what do you reply? The answer is yes, it can happen. For example, if you held:

♠ KQJ4
♥ KQJ75
♦ KQ
♣ KQ

and heard your partner open one heart, there is little point in bidding anything other than a direct 4NT for all you want to know is how many aces he holds. Should he hold all four, then you can count thirteen winners and can settle confidently in 7NT. The way that partner shows all four aces in reply to a Blackwood enquiry is by bidding five clubs—just the same bid that he makes with no aces. Is there any possible danger of confusion? Hardly. With the last example you ask yourself which is more likely—that partner holds all four aces or that he has opened the bidding on the strength of at most two jacks?

The next example shows the ideal sort of hand for Blackwood. Suppose that you have opened one spade with:

♠ KQ10762
♥ 5
♦ AKQ2
♣ K3

and hear our partner raise to four spades. Now, you would have gone on to four spades ourselves if partner had only been able to raise one spade to two spades so, after his jump to game, you have every reason to suspect that there might be twelve or thirteen tricks available, for you have undisclosed values in reserve. Now, partner may hold any one of the following hands:

(a) ♠ A985	(b) ♠ A985	(c) ♠ AJ95
♥ A732	♥ KQ103	♥ KQ103
♦ 84	♦ 84	♦ 84
♣ A65	♣ A65	♣ QJ10

—all perfectly reasonable raises to game. As all you are interested in is the number of aces he holds (spades have been agreed as trumps) you enquire with 4NT. With (a) he replies five spades (three aces) and you can now count six spade tricks, a heart trick, three diamond tricks and two club tricks. Only twelve tricks? No, not at all—you have no immediate losers and after drawing all of the opponents' trumps you will be able to ruff a diamond on the table for your thirteenth winner. So, after five spades, you bid seven spades. If partner holds (b) and replies five hearts, you know that a vital ace is missing and can stop in six spades. Finally, if he holds (c) and responds five diamonds you know that two aces are missing and (reluctantly) put on the brakes in five spades. It is worth noting that in every case you have the values to develop thirteen tricks but with (b) your opponents have an ace to cash first and with (c) their two aces mean that not even a small slam is possible. In every case, once the Blackwood bidder knows how many aces his partner holds he knows precisely at what level to stop. Sometimes it seems better to think of Blackwood as a way of stopping out of slams rather than a way of bidding them!

Suppose, by contrast, that you had started with:

♠ KQ10762
♥ 54
♦ AKQ3
♣ K

and that the bidding had started as before: 1♠—4♠. This is not a suitable hand for Blackwood. Suppose that you had (mistakenly) tried it and learnt of two aces opposite—you would not know which aces partner held and would be unable to judge the final contract. For example, he might hold:

(a)	♠ A985	or	(b)	♠ A985
	♥ KQ103			♥ QJ103
	♦ 84			♦ 84
	♣ A65			♣ AQJ

With (a) six spades would be an excellent contract—the opponents can take only one trick in hearts—but with (b) the defenders will be able to take the first two tricks in hearts. Which hand has partner got? You do not know, for in each case the sum total of your information is that he likes spades, has the values for game, and possesses two aces.

How to distinguish between these hands will be considered in the section on cue-bidding, but before leaving Blackwood there are a couple of other points to note. The first is that if clubs are the agreed trump suit you have to be a little wary in using Blackwood. Suppose you held:

♠ KQ
♥ 2
♦ KQJ2
♣ AK8743

and heard your opening bid of one club raised to three clubs. Very tempting to launch into Blackwood, but what do you do if partner responds five diamonds (one ace)? There are two aces missing, so you do not want to advance to the six level and the ideal contract would be five clubs. But, oh dear! partner's reply has already taken you past that.

The second point is that a direct raise in no-trumps, when no suit has been agreed, that takes the partnership beyond game, for example *1NT—4NT is quantitative and nothing to do with Blackwood*. It simply says "If you are maximum for your 1NT bid, go on to 6NT; if you were minimum for your 1NT bid you must pass, but 4NT should be safe enough". It is all a question of points. It is a fair bet to try *6NT* if you know your side holds *33-34 points* or more between you and you both have balanced hands. Even with 33 you know that you are not missing two aces for there are only 40 points in the pack. So if the 1NT opening showed 12-14 points you would raise to 4NT with an equally balanced hand and 19-20 points; with 22 points you could raise to 6NT directly and with 25 points (when your partnership would have a *minimum of 37 points* and thus not be missing an ace) you would raise directly to *7NT.*

Cue-bidding

The third approach to slam bidding is altogether more sophisticated than the preceding two routes. Suppose that the bidding starts 1♠—3♠ and the opener now bids, say, four clubs. This carries the following messages:

(a) I am interested in a slam—I think that between us we have the values for something more ambitious than just game.

(b) Unfortunately Blackwood will not help me make a sensible decision about our final contract.

(c) We have agreed spades as trumps so, in no way, am I suggesting an alternative trump suit.

(d) I have first-round control in clubs—the ace or (possibly) a void.

(e) How do you feel about the prospects of a slam, partner? I would value your opinion.

Can you see the essential difference from the other ideas? Bashing commits your side to a slam and partner is not consulted. Blackwood simply asks about the number of aces that partner holds—he is not asked to give an opinion as to whether he is minimum or maximum for his bid, suitable or unsuitable for a slam adventure. A typical hand for this cue-bid (1♠—3♠; 4♣) would be:

♠ AKJ85
♥ 4
♦ QJ10
♣ AKJ5

and partner would have a choice of options available. With, say

♠ Q1074
♥ KQ85
♦ K93
♣ 107

he would have no interest in a slam (minimum and holding no aces) and would quietly return to four spades. But with:

♠ Q1094
♥ Q732
♦ AK2
♣ 63

he will co-operate and show his ace of diamonds with a return cue-bid of four diamonds. Note that he is not obliged to show an ace if he has one, especially if this would mean going past the game level. It is only if he is interested in progress that he will show an ace or a void. It is not just that he has an ace that makes six spades attractive, it is because he has the ace of diamonds and not the ace of hearts. And this distinction would never be made by using Blackwood—that only finds out how many aces partner holds, not which aces.

There are several other points to make about cue-bidding. First, it is customary to show your cheapest control so:

West	East
1 ♠	3 ♠
4 ♦	

would deny first-round control in clubs and

West	East
1 ♥	3 ♥
4 ♦	

would deny controls in both spades and clubs.

Secondly it is possible to show second-round controls (either the king or a singleton) but only if you or your partner have already shown first-round control in that suit. This would be a good example:

West	East
♠ AK1083	♠ QJ54
♥ 6	♥ 972
♦ 752	♦ AKJ7
♣ AKQ5	♣ 87

West	East
1 ♠	3 ♠
4 ♣[1]	4 ♦[2]
5 ♣[3]	5 ♦[4]
6 ♠[5]	Pass

[1] I have the ace of clubs and am interested.
[2] I have the ace of diamonds and so am I.
[3] I also have the king of clubs and, although I do not hold the ace of hearts, I am still interested.
[4] I cannot control the hearts either but I hold the king of diamonds.
[5] As I know that we can lose at most one trick in hearts I am prepared to try for the spade slam.

135

Again, Blackwood would not have helped. One ace, yes, but which ace?

Finally, it is possible to combine Blackwood and cue-bids on the same hands, so

West	East
1 ♠	3 ♠
4 ♣	4 ♦
4NT	

is still Blackwood but at least the opener knows that his partner has a control in diamonds and is interested in a move onward.

18

Stayman

Even if you do not like the idea of playing too many conventions—and in top-class play a well-practised partnership may include dozens of them in their repertoire!—Stayman is a simple device that gains far more than it loses. This is always the test of a worthwhile convention. In other words it is a good weapon to include in your armoury and—even if you decide not to use it—you will often find your opponents employing it and it will be a great help to you to know what it is all about.

The idea was first put forward by a British player (Ewart Kempson), polished by another British player (Jack Marx) and publicised by an American player, Sam Stayman. So guess whose name the convention bears!

The convention is simple and, like Blackwood, often misused. If your partner opens 1NT and there is a pass on your right, a response of two clubs loses its natural meaning (please pass, I do not like no-trumps, we have not got the combined values for game, and making eight tricks with clubs will be an easier proposition than making seven tricks in no-trumps) and asks partner whether his 1NT opening includes four cards in either major suit. First, the mechanics of the convention, then the reasons for using it, and the hands on which it might gainfully be employed.

A response of two clubs to an opening bid of 1NT is conventional and asks if, included in his balanced hand, the opener has a four-card major suit. It is, of course, unlikely (but not impossible) that he has five after his 1NT opening bid. Opener's rebids are straightforward:

Two spades:	my opening bid of 1NT includes a four-card spade suit.
Two hearts:	my opening bid of 1NT includes a four-card heart suit.

137

Two diamonds: my opening bid of 1NT does not include either four spades or four hearts.

Note that the two-diamond rebid, just like the response of two clubs, is conventional and does not promise any particular length in the suit named. Should, and it is quite possible, the opening bid of 1NT includes both four spades and four hearts it really does not matter a scrap which one you show. Some players prefer spades, some hearts but (as we will see) the choice is completely irrelevant.

The reason for using the convention is quite simple—the responder hopes to find a better contract in a major suit than the no-trumps that his partner has suggested. This may be two spades or two hearts rather than 1NT or (at the game level) four spades or four hearts rather than 3NT.

Consider some example hands. With:

♠ 74
♥ KQ86
♦ AQJ4
♣ Q32

you hear your partner open 1NT (12-14 points). You have the values for game but, if partner happens to hold four hearts in his hand, four hearts may be a much sounder contract than 3NT. The problem is, of course, that you cannot bid hearts yourself. Two hearts would suggest a longer suit with no interest in game and would insist on partner passing. Three hearts, although insisting on game, would again promise at least five cards in the suit and would incite partner to support you with only three cards in your suit. Two clubs, on the other hand, will smoke out a 4-4 fit in hearts if it exists. So if the opener held:

♠ A63
♥ J1073
♦ K85
♣ AJ10

you would be able to raise his rebid of two hearts to four hearts—a much better game, in view of the combined weakness in spades, than 3NT.

Just suppose that the opener held both major suits and decided to show his spades first—perhaps with:

♠ A963
♥ J1073
♦ K85
♣ AJ

Over his two spades you bid 3NT but now the opener, who now knows that you have at least one four-card major (else why two clubs?) and that it is not spades, can now convert to four hearts—secure in the knowledge that you have four cards in the suit.

You do not need game-going values in order to respond with a Stayman two clubs. For example, with 11 or 12 points, say:

♠ 84
♥ KQ106
♦ J1075
♣ KQ3

you could initiate a Stayman enquiry in response to 1NT (weak). If the opener rebids two hearts, you are prepared to raise to three hearts—inviting game if the opener is maximum but warning him to pass if he is minimum. And if the response to your enquiry is two spades or two diamonds you can safely go back to 2NT. This carries just the same message as a direct raise of 1NT to 2NT—namely, go on to 3NT if you are maximum for your opening bid, pass if you are minimum.

Does this mean that you need the values to raise 1NT to at least 2NT before you can use Stayman? Not at all—but what is absolutely vital is that you must be able to do something sensible over every one of the opener's possible rebids—two spades, two hearts and two diamonds. It looks tempting to try out your new toy with something like:

♠ KQ74
♥ QJ93
♦ 74
♣ 852

If your partner rebids either two spades or two hearts you pass, of course, and your resting spot is very likely to be an improvement on the 1NT that you might have passed. But what if partner has not got a major suit and replies two diamonds? Disaster lies ahead for you can hardly pass (with only two small diamonds) and converting to 2NT is not going to help. If partner is minimum and passes you are likely to go off (you simply have not got the points) and if he is maximum (when you might have had a chance of eight tricks) he will accept your invitation and press on to an almost certainly doomed game contract of 3NT. So this is a hand where the use of Stayman can easily lead your partnership overboard.

The key thing to remember is: "Can I cope sensibly with all three responses that partner may make?" In the last example there was one possibility—two diamonds—that left you in trouble. Nevertheless some weak hands still lend themselves to an intelligent use of Stayman. For example, with:

♠ J864
♥ J752
♦ J10863
♣ None

what would you reply to 1NT if you had never heard of Stayman? Two diamonds, of course, a weakness take-out insisting on partner passing. You will not necessarily make two diamonds but it is always better to go only one or two off in your contract rather than sit and watch partner go three or four off in 1NT. However, try the effect of a Stayman two clubs instead. What can partner reply—two spades? You pass, delighted. Two hearts? You pass, delighted. Two diamonds? You pass, perhaps not delighted but this is just what you would have bid yourself if not playing Stayman. The only difference is that partner is declarer instead of you!

There are one or two other types of weak hand with which you can 'operate' intelligently. For example:

♠ J9743
♥ QJ75
♦ 6
♣ 842

Without the aid of Stayman you would have bid a dull two spades, but why not try Stayman on the way? Partner may have four hearts and, by passing his response, you may well have found a better resting spot than two spades. As always, you must ask yourself what you will do over all of partner's possible replies. Over two hearts, you pass. Over two spades, you pass. And over the depressing bid of two diamonds? You bid two spades and, just as in the previous example, you are no worse off than if you were not playing Stayman.

Just as a matter of revision, suppose you are dealt:

♠ AQ743
♥ 5
♦ AK72
♣ J105

141

and hear partner open 1NT (12-14 points). What do you respond? *Not* a Stayman two clubs for this is designed to discover 4-4 fits. With this hand you do not wish to find out if partner holds four spades, you want to know if he holds three or more. You respond three spades, forcing to game, and he will raise you to four spades if he has. Should he have only two spades, he will rebid 3NT and you will probably be better there than anywhere else in spite of your singleton heart.

It is certainly worth mentioning that you can also use Stayman by bidding three clubs in reply to an opening bid of 2NT (showing a balanced 20-22 points). There are alternative methods on the market but the simplest idea is to bid in exactly the same way as over an opening bid of 1NT—but one level higher, of course. For example:

West	East
♠ AQ73	♠ KJ64
♥ A52	♥ 63
♦ KQJ4	♦ 1093
♣ A9	♣ J1042

As you can see, a contract of 3NT could easily fail if a defender with five hearts also holds the ace of diamonds, but four spades stands a much better chance—there will be only one heart trick to lose.

The bidding would go:

West	East
2NT	3 ♣
3 ♠	4 ♠

Remember, you only need 4 or 5 points to go on to game facing a 2NT opening bid and that any response, including Stayman, commits the partnership to bidding game. The only way to put on the brakes, facing a 2NT opening, is to pass.

19

Interference

All of our discussions about bidding so far have been on the assumption that the opponents remain silent and you and your partner have a clear run to what you hope will be your best contract. Real life is not like that—often the other side join in, sometimes inconveniently, and matters become more difficult.

The time has come to consider what action you can take after one of the opponents has opened the bidding. There are a number of possibilities open to you, everything depending on the type of hand you have been dealt. To start with we will assume that there has been an opening bid of one diamond on your right.

I Simple overcall

This is one of the most valuable, and yet most misused, weapons in the bidding war. The important fact to master is that overcalls and opening bids have different purposes and are frequently based on completely different hands. *Opening bids promise points; overcalls promise the ability to win tricks if the overcaller's suit is trumps.*

Compare these two hands:

(a)   ♠ KQ10973   (b)   ♠ A973
      ♥ 64   ♥ A64
      ♦ A82   ♦ J82
      ♣ 74   ♣ A74

You would not make an opening bid with (a) but it is an eminently sound overcall of one spade over one club, one diamond or one heart. Even if you find partner with absolutely nothing, you will come to five or even six tricks in a spade contract. Indeed, it would be a pleasure to do so for if the opponents have the rest of the high cards and are prepared to leave you in one spade, they will have missed an easy game.

The advantages of joining in are many—you pave the way for competing in the auction if partner can support your suit, you cramp your opponents' style, and you suggest a good lead to partner if you end up defending.

For an overcall you need a good five-card suit (or longer), so your partner can support with only three cards in your suit. A 'good' suit is difficult to define, but it is interesting to note that a suit of KQJ109 (6 points) guarantees four tricks if it trumps but if your suit is AK432 (7 points) you can only be absolutely sure of two tricks.

The most favourable time to overcall is when you are not vulnerable and can show your suit at the one level. At the other end of the scale, if you are vulnerable (when the penalties for failure are more severe) and you have to bid at the two level in order to show your suit, you need some extra values—perhaps a sixth card in your suit.

Contrast this with hand (b). An opening bid, yes, but not an overcall. You might easily end with only three tricks if you find your partner with nothing.

II Take-out double

Sometimes you find yourself with the values for an opening bid but no long suit—perhaps:

♠ KJ74
♥ AJ93
♦ 4
♣ A1085

You are all set to open one club when you hear one diamond on your right. Certainly you want to join in for if partner has length in any of your three suits you might make a lot of tricks. Yet you have no good five-card suit and no desire to put all of your eggs in one basket. The solution is to say *"Double"*. As you will appreciate, the normal meaning of a double is an attempt to punish the opponents by increasing the stakes when you think that they are out of their depth. *Here the use of double is conventional. The message that you convey is that you have the values for an opening bid, are relatively short in the suit that your opponent has named, and have reasonable support for the other three suits.* The hand illustrated above is perfect in every respect, but you would not worry too much if perhaps you held one diamond more and one card less in one of the other suits.

The take-out double introduces several new aspects into the bidding. For example, consider how East should respond after the bidding has started:

West	North	East	South
			1 ♦
Double	Pass	?	

The first point to note is that, even with a terrible hand, he is expected to respond. So with:

♠ 103
♥ 10874
♦ J95
♣ 9762

he cannot pass and hope for the best, for the worst, almost inevitably, will happen—one diamond doubled will make with three or four overtricks and that will prove very expensive for East-West. No, East has to dredge up a reply of one heart (here his cheapest four-card suit) but now, as the partnership should have located a trump suit with eight cards between them, the roof is unlikely to fall in and any loss should be small. A word of warning to West, though. If your double elicits a simple response like this, *always bear in mind that you forced partner to bid—and he may well have virtually nothing.*

Having in mind the sort of hand on which East was bound to reply, what should he do with a reasonable hand? Say:

♠ Q3
♥ K10876
♦ 9763
♣ KJ

The answer is to jump to two hearts, encouraging but not committing the partnership to game. With an even better hand, say:

♠ AQ
♥ K108762
♦ 97
♣ Q85

he should take all the strain from his partner by jumping immediately to the game in hearts—it is difficult to construct a sensible take-out double for West which will not offer an excellent play for four hearts.

A fair guide is to make a simple reply with 0-8 points, jump with 9-11 points, and insist on a game with more.

You can reply in no-trumps to partner's double, too, but remember that he has advertised a shortage in the opponent's suit, so you should have their suit well guarded before preferring no-trumps to a suit. Clearly, you can respond 1NT, 2NT or 3NT according to the strength of your hand—just imagine that partner has opened the bidding which, in effect, he has.

Having stressed, we hope sufficiently, that you should never pass partner's take-out double, we have to admit that you can do so, although it will be rare that you have the right hand. For example with

♠ A2
♥ 103
♦ KQJ1043
♣ Q85

you would be delighted to pass partner's double of one diamond!

The next point to note is that if the opener's partner bids over the double, the doubler's partner is no longer *forced* to reply. So after:

West	North	East	South
1♦	Double	1♠	?

the contract is no longer one diamond doubled but an ordinary one spade. South will certainly bid if he has something worthwhile to show, but is relieved of the obligation to bid with rubbish.

Finally, there is the chance of ambiguity as to the meaning of a double. Is it for take-out, or is it for penalties? In the simplest case (a double of an opening bid of one of a suit on your right) there is no question about it—it is for take-out. On grounds of frequency it is much more useful for the bid to have this meaning for it would be extremely rarely that, without yet having heard anything from your partner, you would be in a position to want to savage an opponent at the one level. The trouble arises in other situations.

The following guidelines will solve the problem (most of the time!).

(a) A double of a no-trump contract is always for penalties. (You cannot have good support for all four suits!) The more points your partner has, the happier he is to pass. He will only remove your double with a weak hand and a long suit.

(b) If your partner has made a bid (other than pass) a double by you is for penalties.

(c) If the opponents have bid three (or four) suits, any double is for penalties.

Test yourself on these auctions.

(1)	**West**	**North**	**East**	**South**
	1♣	Pass	1♥	Double

(2)	**West**	**North**	**East**	**South**
	Pass	1♥	1NT	Double

(3)	**West**	**North**	**East**	**South**
				1♥
	1♠	Pass	Pass	Double

(4)	**West**	**North**	**East**	**South**
				Pass
	1♣	Pass	1♠	Double

(1) Take-out. South is interested in diamonds and spades.
(2) Penalties. Partner has bid *and* they are in no-trumps.
(3) Take-out. South has a good opening bid with not only hearts but fair support for both diamonds and clubs as well.
(4) Take-out. South is interested in hearts and diamonds. Note that he is just short of an opening bid for he passed initially.

III Jump overcall
Sometimes you find yourself with quite a good hand, unsuitable for a double as most of your strength lies in a six-card suit. Perhaps:

♠ K3
♥ AKQ1086
♦ 74
♣ A65

which is altogether too good for a simple overcall (partner will never imagine that your hand is so strong). The solution is to make *a jump overcall—one level higher than necessary.* So with the above hand you would bid two hearts over one diamond or three hearts over one spade. The bid is strong, suggesting seven or eight playing tricks, but does not force partner to respond.

IV 1NT overcall

Overcalling always carries some risk of being sandwiched between two opponents with good hands. When you overcall in a suit you have the security of trump length; when you make a take-out double you have the safety factor of offering partner the choice of suits in which to play.

When you overcall in no-trumps, however, you will have no long suit and no distribution. The only thing that can help you is the possession of high cards. This is why, although an opening bid of 1NT is based on 12-14 points, an overcall of 1NT should contain a firm *15-17 points in a balanced hand with a good guard in the opponent's suit*—the suit that is likely to be led against you. So over one diamond bid 1NT with:

♠ K74
♥ A83
♦ AQ7
♣ A983

Partner treats this just as though you had opened 1NT, showing 15-17 points.

V Pre-emptive overcall

This is just like a pre-emptive opening bid, showing a good seven-card suit with very little outside. It is designed, purely and simply, to annoy the opponents! So, over one diamond, with:

(a)   ♠ KQJ9863   and   (b)   ♠ KQJ109863
                   ♥ 5   ♥ 5
                   ♦ J82   ♦ J82
                   ♣ 105   ♣ 10

bid three spades and four spades respectively.

Note well that *a pre-emptive overcall is made at least two levels higher than necessary*. Over one diamond, one spade is a simple overcall, two spades is a jump overcall, while three spades and four spades are pre-emptive. Over one heart, though, if you plan to bid diamonds, two diamonds is a simple overcall, three diamonds is a jump overcall (strong) while four diamonds is pre-emptive.

VI Unusual 2NT

Most players would be a great deal better off (financially!) if they had never heard of this weapon. The idea is reasonable but it is usually misapplied in practice. Only if you and your partner have discussed it, of course, an overcall of a major suit with 2NT shows considerable length in both minor suits. It is usually played as a weak call, suggesting a possible cheap sacrifice against a major suit game. So, over one spade or one heart, 2NT would show perhaps:

                     ♠ 3
                     ♥ 5
                     ♦ KJ1097
                     ♣ AJ10863

As we say, it is not a great weapon, but it is useful to know about it in case it is employed by your opponents.

VII Bid the opponent's suit

First, a question. What would you open with:

♠ AKQ74
♥ AKJ106
♦ 2
♣ AQ

Two clubs, we hope, for the hand is well worth insisting on game. To your annoyance, however, the hand on your right opens one diamond. You can no longer bid two clubs—that would be a simple overcall showing clubs. You could start with a double but your partner will never imagine that you are as strong as this. The solution is to bid the opponent's suit, so, over one diamond, bid two diamonds. This does *not*, repeat *not*, show diamonds—it tells your partner that you have something approaching a conventional two-club opening. Partner has no conventional negative but you both have to keep on bidding until you have reached a game.

VIII Pass

One of the most overlooked bids in bridge. Obviously you pass if you have a bad hand, but you should also pass if you have length and strength in the suit opened on your right. So, over one diamond, with:

♠ 3
♥ AKJ
♦ AQ1073
♣ J764

you have an automatic pass. And not only pass, but pass smoothly—do not brood for ages before finally and reluctantly passing. The reason for inaction is quite simple—the hand has all the earmarks of a misfit for both sides and you would prefer your opponents to play it. If you bid, more often than not you end up with a minus score. If you pass, more often than not you end up with a plus score.

Whatever you do, do not double (you are sure you hear your partner jump in spades); do not bid 1NT (yes, you have the right number of points but the wrong shape), and do not dream of bidding two diamonds—we have just discussed in the preceding section what that would mean. Grit your teeth and pass!

IX Protection

In view of the fact that the second player to speak may be forced to pass with quite good values, it is a good idea to take action (whenever possible) in the fourth seat if the opening bid has been followed by two passes.

West	North	East	South
1 ♦	Pass	Pass	?

The point to remember is that your partner should have *some* values for, otherwise, why have the opponents stopped at the one level?

South's bid, if he makes one, is said to be *protective*, and a sensible rule is that you should do something with possibly 3 points less than you would have done in the second position. So:

West	North	East	South
1 ♦	Pass	Pass	1NT

would suggest only 11-14 points, whilst a *take-out double* (with all the right distribution) might be made with as little as 9 or 10 points.

> ♠ K764
> ♥ A853
> ♦ 2
> ♣ Q1087

would be enough for a take-out double if one diamond is passed round to you. Now, if partner had passed because he has length and strength in diamonds, he may pass your take-out double for penalties, and you might well collect a big score.

20

Optional Extras

These are a few bidding ideas that are quite popular. It is not at all necessary to adopt them yourself but it is nice to know about them in case they are included in your opponents' methods.

I Five-card majors

Every so often you will find that your opponents are playing 'five-card majors'. All that this means is that when they open the bidding with one spade or one heart they guarantee at least five cards in the suit named. (It is only the opening bid to which this refers, so 1♦—1♥ does not promise more than four hearts. Equally, 1♦—1♥ —1♠ does not promise more than four spades.) The method has its advantages and its disadvantages—the main drawback is that sometimes an opening bid of one of a minor suit has to be based on only a three-card suit. For example, with:

```
♠ AQ74
♥ KJ93
♦ Q74
♣ J5
```

and playing a strong no-trump, there is no alternative to opening one diamond. (A bid of one club with only a two-card suit would be even worse!) And again, with:

```
♠ AQ74
♥ AK63
♦ J5
♣ Q94
```

153

and playing a weak no-trump there would be nothing left but to open one club. It is true that the partner of the opener can raise a major suit with only three-card support but, especially if the bidding is competitive, he may be reluctant to support a minor suit even with four cards in the suit himself.

II Weak twos

The opening bids of two of a suit that we have discussed have all been strong bids suggesting eight or nine playing tricks or (in the case of clubs) a game-going hand. Some partnerships prefer to use opening bids of two spades and two hearts as weak bids, not quite as weak as a pre-emptive opening but suggesting a good six-card suit in a hand just short of an opening bid of one. Typical examples would be:

♠ KQ10974	or	♠ 76
♥ 63		♥ KQJ975
♦ K85		♦ QJ2
♣ 42		♣ 103

to be opened two spades and two hearts respectively.

If you hear a weak two bid by an opponent it is sensible to treat it as a one bid—in other words suit overcalls are natural, a double is for take-out and 2NT shows a strong balanced hand with a good guard in their suit. Yes, you have to take action a level higher than over an opening bid of one—but that is why your opponents are playing weak twos!

It is worth noting that pairs who employ these weak twos often assign artificial meanings to their opening bids of both two clubs and two diamonds. Two clubs (with the usual negative reply of two diamonds) and followed by a bid in any of the four suits shows eight or nine playing tricks in the suit names on the second round; two diamonds (with the negative reply of two hearts) takes over the role of the forcing-to-game bid of two clubs. This scheme is often known as Benjamin or Benjaminised Acol.

III Transfers

A number of partnerships play that some responses to 1NT (and 2NT) are transfers—in other words not showing the suit named but asking partner to bid the suit ranking immediately above it. A response of two clubs to 1NT is still Stayman but a response of two diamonds asks the opener to bid two hearts, and a response of two hearts asks him to bid two spades. This idea, often described as 'simple transfers', is not uncommon and you may meet pairs who take the idea still further with a response of two spades showing clubs and a response of 2NT showing diamonds.

It all sounds completely pointless but in fact the idea has considerable merit. For example, suppose that you have a reasonably balanced hand containing five hearts and the values to invite game by raising your partner's opening bid of 1NT to 2NT. Playing traditional methods you are left with the choice of responding two hearts (over which your partner will not bid again), three hearts (which insists on game being reached whether partner is minimum or not), or 2NT (expressing your values accurately but not telling partner that you have five hearts). This is a problem which is neatly solved by playing transfers. You respond two diamonds to 1NT, forcing partner to bid two hearts. Then you go back to 2NT and have given a perfect description of your hand (five hearts, happy enough with no-trumps, but not quite sure whether you have the combined values for game). Partner passes, bids 3NT, bids three hearts or bids four hearts according to whether he is minimum or maximum for his 1NT bid and whether (with three or more hearts in his hand) he judges that the hand will be better played with hearts as trumps.

Always remember that you must *alert immediately* your partner makes a conventional bid, a bid that does not have its normal meaning. These alertable bids include transfers and weak twos, and opening bids of one diamond or one club if you are playing five-card majors. This is usually done by rapping smartly on the table, after which the opponent whose turn it is to bid is entitled, though not obliged, to ask the partner of the bidder what they understand by the bid.

21

Duplicate Bridge

Bridge can be played in two distinct ways—what is usually described as rubber bridge, where four people play for money stakes (even if it is only 1p per 100!) and duplicate bridge, where only honour is at stake. Do not be alarmed! We are not going to describe a completely different game, and everything that we have said so far applies equally to both forms of the game. All that the switch from one to the other involves are one or two minor changes in the scoring and a slightly different procedure.

The essence of duplicate bridge is to avoid the luck element of being dealt good hands or bad hands. In its commonest form, a pairs competition, there are at least three tables (there may be far more) each with its complement of four players. All of the partnerships remained unchanged throughout the session. The luck element is eliminated by ensuring that all of the competitors play exactly the same hands and it will be a question of which pair does best. If you seem to hold poor cards you do not have to worry, for all the players against whom you are competing will be playing (sooner or later) with the same poor cards.

The difference in the playing procedure is that the cards are stored in wallets or boards, each of which has four pockets, one for each of the four hands of one deal. The wallet is clearly marked with the dealer and the vulnerability to be assumed when the deal is played (Love All, North-South game; East-West game, or Game All). The first time a hand is played (and only the first time!) the cards are shuffled and dealt in the normal fashion.

The play is slightly different in that when the four cards to a trick are played each player keeps his own card in from of him. The centre of the table is never used, all four players ending each deal with their own thirteen cards neatly lined up along their own edge of the table. A count of the tricks won and lost by your side is kept by pointing the length of each card toward your partner (as it is turned over) for each trick won by your side; and pointing towards your opponents for each trick lost by your side. Thus at any time—and especially at the end—you can see immediately how many tricks have been won and lost by each side. As you turn your cards over keep them in line, working from left to right, so that it is very easy to reconstruct the play in the event of a possible query.

At the end of each hand, after the score has been agreed, you take particular care that your thirteen cards (no more, no less!) are carefully returned to the appropriate pocket of the wallet.

The usual arrangement is that after playing a set of, perhaps, three boards, you pass the completed hands to another table and prepare to meet a new pair of opponents. In charge of the whole operation is the tournament director who will tell you when and where to move and where to put the completed boards. If all goes according to plan, at the end of the session you will have played all of the hands in circulation and met a cross-section of the other pairs as opponents. The tournament director will also score the event overall, but to do this he has to have all of the results available—and this is where the minor scoring changes referred to above are important.

Each hand that you play is a separate entity—there is nothing carried forward to the next, and there is no distinction between above and below the line as there is in rubber bridge. There are three extra bonuses to be scored—500 points for bidding and making a vulnerable game (remember, the vulnerability is marked on the wallet and there is no longer any rubber to be won); 300 points for bidding and making a non-vulnerable game; and 50 points for bidding and making any part-score. A few examples will make this clear.

i) Vulnerable, you bid four spades and make eleven tricks. You score 120 points for your four spades, 30 for the overtrick, and 500 for the vulnerable game. Total score +650 points.

ii) Non-vulnerable, you bid six diamonds and make twelve tricks. You score 120 for six diamonds, the usual 500 for bidding and making a non-vulnerable slam, and 300—the extra bonus—for making a non-vulnerable game. Total score 920 points.

iii) At love all, you bid three clubs and make eleven tricks. You score 60 for three clubs, 40 for the overtricks and 50 for making a part-score. Total 150 points.

Each board contains what is called a travelling scoresheet—which you only look at after playing the hand! On it, one of the four players at your table will enter the score that you have just achieved and you can compare it with the scores collected by those of your competitors who have already played the hand.

A traveller might look like this:

N-S Pair	E-W Pair	Contract	Result	N-S	E-W
1	6	4♠	+1	450	
2	9	4♠	=	420	
3	7	3NT	−1		50
4	10	3NT	−2		100
5	8	4♠	=	420	

Although you do not have to worry about it (it is the tournament director's responsibility) the scoring works like this:

Pair 1 have the best of all the North-South scores—they score 2 matchpoints for every North-South pair whose score they have bettered and 1 matchpoint for every North-South pair whose score they have equalled. So they collect 8 matchpoints. Pairs 2 and 5 did next best among the North-Souths—beating two other North-South pairs and tying with each other. So they collect 5 matchpoints each. Pair 3, in losing 50 points, did better than Pair 4 who lose 100 points, and so Pair 3 collect 2 matchpoints. We will leave you to work out what Pair 4 scored!

The East-West pairs, of course, score the complement of their North-South opponents. In other words, matching Pair 4's zero score, the opponents (Pair 10) score best of the East-West pairs and collect 8 matchpoints.

One of the intriguing things about this form of bridge is that all the hands are equally important. Making one more trick than everyone else in a contract of one club scores just as many matchpoints as if you were the only pair to bid and make a spectacular grand slam—it is doing *better* than your competitors as frequently as possible that counts.

In rubber bridge, if you bid four spades and make only nine tricks, you are never quite sure what went wrong. Half the fun of duplicate is being able to compare your score with others. If everybody else also made nine tricks but had stopped in two spades or three spades you can conclude that your bidding was too optimistic. If, on the other hand, everybody else has also bid four spades but you were the only one to go down, everything points to a misjudgement by you in the play of the cards.

Duplicate is a wonderful way to improve your game!

By now you should be well on your way to understanding the principles of bridge, and to enjoying a lifetime of pleasure and challenge from this most rewarding of games. Don't worry if you didn't grasp everything at the first reading—you can always return later to anything which puzzled you. There is no substitute for actual play, and any problem areas will almost certainly seem as clear as daylight when you have gained a little more experience at the table.

Have fun!